BRIERFIELD
Plantation Home of Jefferson Davis

BRIERFIELD: "THE HOUSE THAT JEFF BUILT"
1863 or 1865 when occupied by Union troops

J. Mack Moore Collection, Old Courthouse Museum, Vicksburg, Mississippi

BRIERFIELD

PLANTATION HOME
OF
JEFFERSON DAVIS

by

FRANK E. EVERETT, JR.

UNIVERSITY AND COLLEGE PRESS OF MISSISSIPPI
SOUTHERN STATION, BOX 5164
HATTIESBURG, MISSISSIPPI 39401
1971

DEDICATED
TO
ALL THOSE WHO HAVE HELPED
AND ENCOURAGED

Preface and Acknowledgments

OF THE HUNDREDS of plantation dwellings built in the South during the decades before the Civil War, none has had richer associations with men and history than *Brierfield*, home of Jefferson and Varina Davis. Involved as it was with the aspirations and daily lives of its owners, the house was in a very special sense the tangible record of their personal victories and defeats. From the vantage point of time, the history of *Brierfield* takes on an even wider significance. It becomes, in fact, a symbol of the public and private aspects of Southern living throughout almost a century. War, flood, and fire have destroyed most of the physical evidences of *Brierfield*, but its significance in Southern history continues to be felt. To maintain the record, to recreate the atmosphere in which the dwelling was conceived, and to trace its rise, prosperity, and physical dissolution have been the primary objectives of this work.

So much of the external record was destroyed in

the fire which burned *Brierfield* to the foundation stones that the preparation of this book would have been impossible without the assistance of a number of persons who have generously given of their technical knowledge, family records, and personal memories. Adequate acknowledgment of my debt to all of them I cannot make in a brief statement, but to them I wish to express my gratitude. Among those who have directly assisted me in establishing the history of *Brierfield*, I wish to thank the following persons:

Dr. Hudson Strode, whose volumes about Jefferson Davis have been a resource of inestimable value.

Members of the Davis family, including Mr. Jefferson Hayes-Davis, grandson of Jefferson Davis; Mr. Albert Franklin Ganier, great grandson of Amanda Davis, sister of Jefferson Davis; Mrs. Beulah Smith (Mrs. Rhea N.) Watts and Mr. John B. Stirling, Jr., descendants of Anna Davis Smith, another of Jefferson's sisters; and Mrs. Julia F. (Mrs. Best) Montfort, for their help in establishing genealogical relationships and sharing their memories of *Brierfield*.

Mrs. Henry Bobb, who lived at Brierfield while her husband was manager, and the daughter of Mr. A. B. Couvillon, who resided in the house for many years while her father was manager of the plantation, as well as Mrs. Harry Doyle and Mrs. James D. Hitt, who both taught at *Brierfield* during the early years of the twentieth century, for sharing with me their recollections of *Brierfield*. Mr. James (Jim) Barnett, who was born on the Davis property about eighty years ago and has known *Brierfield* all his life, for his accounts of the floods of the 'twenties as well as the burning of *Brierfield*.

Mr. Victor Bobb of Vicksburg, who spent much time on Davis Island when his cousin Henry Bobb was manager of *Brierfield* in the early twenties. He observed the house closely with a good practical builder's eye, made notes, and has generously shared his invaluable information.

Mr. V. Blaine Russell, Judge Ben A. Guider, Mr. J. Cyril O'Neill, Mrs. Harry Ballinger, Mrs. Celeste Hyland Newell, Miss Clara Stevens, Mrs. Lily Hunter Pennebaker, Mr. Cary Pennebaker, Mrs. Salome N. Brady, Miss Mary Louise Cashman, Miss Frances Crawford, and Mrs. Laura D. S. Harrell, who made available to me records, photographs, and letters relating to *Brierfield*.

Mrs. Mary Frances Murphree Ford, Senator Mitchell Robinson, Mr. and Mrs. Walker Burnside, Mr. William G. Beanland, and Mr. John Dale, Jr., who in various ways made possible my research on Davis Island.

Senator John Stennis and Governor John Bell Williams, then a member of Congress, for assistance in searching for information about *Brierfield* in the files of the National Archives and the Library of Congress.

Preface and Acknowledgments

I especially wish to thank Dr. R. A. McLemore, Director of the Mississippi Department of Archives and History, who read the manuscript; Mrs. Dora B. Williams, whose inquiries prompted the author's determination to write the history of *Brierfield*; and Mrs. Maxine M. Fowler, who rendered the many services and skills of a cheerful and talented secretary. Most of all, I thank my wife, Clyde Bryant Everett, who has enthusiastically encouraged the research and patiently counseled with me through the writing of the manuscript.

Table of Contents

BRIERFIELD
Plantation Home of Jefferson Davis

CHAPTER I

From Today to Yesterday

A VISITOR TO Davis Island today finds a vast expanse of green timbered wilderness slashed occasionally by the gleaming scimitars of half-hidden lakes and open areas of brown loam land slowly giving way to the persistent wild growth which struggles to reclaim the rich ridges where Joseph and Jefferson Davis once cultivated acres of cotton when the area was known as Davis Bend. Around this secluded island lies the great oval lasso of Palmyra Lake, now a placid remnant of the turbulent Mississippi River that embraced these fertile acres more than a hundred years ago. In 1867, like a huge guillotine detaching the head from the body, the swirling river separated the island from the mainland when it cut the narrow neck of the original peninsula and paralyzed time for a century.

At the far western edge of the loop, only a heavy cluster of giant oaks marks the site where Joseph Davis built the plantation mansion *Hurricane*, which formerly presided over all of these acres. Today in the south central part of the island stand the empty brick pillars which once supported Jefferson Davis' home, *Brierfield*. In this quiet and remote spot one feels an overwhelming awe and imagines the presence of those who once walked and worked in this very place. The stillness filters deep inside and generates excitement, but there is no sense of peace. The silent conflict rages as nature counterattacks the clearings and frontiers once established and maintained by the Davis brothers. The brambles are returning.

Between the small grassy airplane landing strip (which affords the easiest access to the island) and the former home site extends the old, tightly packed, sandy road which once connected the Davis land to Vicksburg. Down a straight stretch of the roadway—a perfect track—Jefferson and Varina Davis gaily rode and raced their favorite horses. Today there are only the dainty cloven prints of deer and the occasional glimpse of a covey of brown quail.

On an old fence bordering the south edge of the road, a long hedgerow of wild roses rambles untended and untrained. One wonders whether they may be the undisciplined descendants of the *Brierfield* roses that Jefferson and Varina Davis were trimming in February, 1861, when a breathless rider from Vicksburg urged his lathered horse over this very road to bring news of Davis' selection as President of the Confederacy. The entrance to the house must have been near the point where the message was delivered.

From Today to Yesterday

From a heavy tangle of vines and dense growth protrude the bare, broken chimneys and foundations of *Brierfield*. Only the massive yard trees and the tumbled brick remain. Three old topless cisterns, like old soldiers reluctant to die, stand faithful duty behind the scant remnants of the vanished home they once served.

In the twentieth century, access to Davis Island is not easy. Water and a deep layer of forest surround the old home sites. The land, privately owned and used primarily as a game preserve, is not open to the public. The present owners, however, are most courteous and considerate to persons who for valid reasons wish to visit the site.

The short plane flight from the Vicksburg airport requires less than ten minutes. Although there is no ground transportation on the island, *Brierfield* is only a short walk from the landing strip. If the visitor comes by boat across the river or Palmyra Lake, however, he must endure much difficult walking in order to reach the mid-portion of the island. If the weather is good and the water low, and if proper arrangements have been made in advance, a visitor may cross Palmyra Lake on a small private ferry operated at irregular intervals from the extreme western perimeter. Another private ferry is sometimes available from Louisiana at the northern side of the island.

The Vicksburg airport, located on the shelf between the Mississippi hills and the river, is 111 feet above sea level. Nearer the stream, the land slopes gently to about 75 feet. The rich and productive Louisiana cattle and farm lands to the west rise between 75 and 85 feet above sea level. By comparison, the former Davis land ranges somewhat higher in the alluvial plain at 80 to 85 feet; and the well-drained, sandy loam cotton land is as good as any other along the river—perhaps even better.[1]

In 1867, as the result of an avulsion known as the "Davis Cut-Off," Davis Bend became an island west of the mainstream of the Mississippi River. More recently, in 1933, Diamond Point Cut-off further east replaced the original Davis Cut-off, retaining but enlarging the island and increasing its isolation and remoteness. Accretion and filling around the outer circumference have virtually concealed Hurricane Island at the west end and Palmyra Island on the north. Since 1940, a sweeping curve of the river has cut severely into the southeast part of the island to within a mile from *Brierfield*. A shoreline revetment constructed by the United States Engineers has, hopefully, now stabilized the crumbling bank. Thus, over the years, the great Mississippi River has played several capricious tricks with the Davis property, accelerating its reversion to a semi-wilderness such as existed when Joseph Davis first entered the bend.

[1] Elevations and river information have been supplied by the Mississippi River Commission and U.S. Corps of Engineers, Vicksburg District.

CHAPTER II

Davis Bend and Hurricane

JOSEPH E. DAVIS, eldest brother of Jefferson Davis, was a prominent member of the convention which met at Washington, in Adams County, during July, 1817, to write a constitution and form a state government for Mississippi. One of the leading lawyers of his time, Joseph Davis had established a substantial law practice in old Greenville, Jefferson County. After contributing his talents to the creation of Mississippi's statehood, he returned to the further improvement of his personal fortune. On May 18, 1818, less than a year after the convention, he acquired from the United States extensive acreage in Township 14 North, Range 1 West, Warren County, Mississippi. The land lay within a sweeping curve of the Mississippi River, that turned westward fifteen miles south of the future site of Vicksburg, which was not founded until 1819.

The patents were issued to Joseph E. Davis and Littleton Henderson, who assigned his interest inside the bend to Davis. Of the 11,000 acres in the peninsula, Joseph obtained an extensive bloc of about 6,900 acres in the choice western and southern parts, including most of the river frontage. Before long this encircled expanse of fine cotton land became known to rivermen as "Davis Bend." Although Joseph sold part of the land to such friends as General John A. Quitman, he reserved to himself 5,280 acres where he eventually raised annually hundreds of bales of cotton.

For the next few years Joseph E. Davis was busy attending to his large law practice in Greenville and Natchez. During 1821, he was instrumental in organizing the Mississippi Bar Association, the first in the nation; and after serving on its executive committee for three years, he became its president in 1824. Because he was occupied with his profession, Joseph assigned to his brother Isaac the formidable task of managing the clearing and development of the property at Davis Bend. Their father, Samuel Davis, had fallen upon bad times and to pay a debt assumed for his son-in-law had to sell his property in Wilkinson County to Joseph. In July, 1824, on a trip upriver to the Bend, Samuel Davis became ill and died. He was buried in a grove of oaks near the plantation headquarters.

In 1827, when he was forty-three years old, Joseph Davis married Eliza Van Bentheson of New Orleans. She was only sixteen.[1] Joseph had begun to build a

[1] The memorial inscription on the Joseph Davis monument in the Davis graveyard at *Hurricane* shows Eliza Davis' date of birth as June 23, 1811.

comfortable home at the west end of the Bend, and after his marriage to Eliza settled there with his bride and three daughters from a previous union[2] (Florida, born in 1817; Caroline, 1819; and Mary, 1821). While the building was being constructed, a devastating cyclone in 1824 had demolished part of the main house and killed the infant son of Isaac and Susannah Davis. During the storm, Isaac had suffered a broken leg which crippled him for life. The young parents were so shaken by this tragedy that they bought a farm and moved to another location, where they would not encounter so many sad reminders of happier days. Because of the great storm, the Davises named the plantation home *Hurricane.*

Varina Howell Davis, Jefferson's second wife, has recorded her memories of the mansion at *Hurricane.*[3] Set amidst wide lawns and surrounded by enormous oaks and trees brought from Europe, the house stood in isolated grandeur—rambling, misshapen in appearance, surrounded by rank, luxurious nature. Above a heavy roof, its many sharp, pointed dormers glistened like spires. The house stood three stories high and afforded a fine view of the Mississippi River from its high windows. The center structure of *Hurricane* was

---

[2] Hudson Strode, *Jefferson Davis: American Patriot* (New York: Harcourt, Brace and Company, 1955), p. 51.

[3] Varina Howell Davis, *Jefferson Davis, Ex-President of the Confederate States, A Memoir by His Wife* (2 vols.; New York: Belford Company, Publishers, 1890), I, 192–194.

nearly surrounded upstairs and down by wide galleries. The lower floor was paved with bricks which servants reddened industriously. The great house gave
an impression of size and solidarity; and although
devoid of architectural grace, it did possess a certain
dignity. Mrs. M. P. H. Roach, who was a frequent
visitor to *Hurricane* during 1845 and 1846, has also
recorded her impressions of the mansion.[4] She remembered that the carriage approach to the front of the
house, which faced the river, followed a very long
circular drive, lined and shaded by fine oaks. Due west
in front of the mansion, a long walk led through the
circle of oaks to the front gates and finally to the
warehouse and boat landing on the river. The intervening grassy lawn beneath pecan and oak trees created
a pleasant approach to the house from the river.

The main part of the building was constructed of
brick, and the walls were sturdy and thick with many
windows—small in proportion to the size of the house.
The lower part of each door was panelled, and the upper portion consisted of six small panes of glass. The
interior of the center part of the building had low
ceilings with a wide hall dividing the four rooms on the
lower floor. The second story and the attic also contained four spacious rooms each.

[4] Mrs. M. P. H. Roach, memorandum dated August 22, 1897,
deposited in the Department of Archives and History, Jackson,
Mississippi.

The drawing room and the tea room, where the ladies gathered, were located on the first floor to the right of the center hall. On the left were Joseph Davis' bedroom (adjoined by a small storeroom where he kept a variety of choice surprises for servants, children, and guests) and his office, where he and Jefferson often rested after riding their plantations. Here the brothers' conversations ranged broadly over many diverse subjects. They exchanged ideas concerning local plantation affairs and agricultural experiments in which they used scientific farming methods quite advanced for their time. They also discussed books, law, and current events, particularly political matters.

A large annex, forty-three feet long and twenty-five feet wide, extended to the west of the main structure. The dining room, paved with bricks in cement, was located at the ground level in this addition. Above it was a large area with a high arched ceiling, fireplace, many-paned windows, and walls lined with family portraits. Here in the "Music Room" young people congregated to sing, play games, act charades, and stage mock concerts. A paved walk at ground level and a covered way from the upstairs gallery provided access from the main building to the dining room-music room annex. Directly behind this annex was a brick house for kitchen and laundry, with bedrooms above for the house servants. Trained mechanics had provided running water for the bathrooms in the mansion from a large attic tank pumped full each morning by servants.[5]

A little southwest from the main house stood a well-proportioned, classic cottage surrounded by squared Doric columns. This "garden cottage" contained bachelor quarters which were used when the big house was full.

A large garden consisting of several acres spread to the rear of the house. Here native flowers of all kinds, as well as rare roses and shrubs, grew abundantly, surrounded by a natural hedge of roses, honeysuckle, and jasmine. The garden was flanked by eight acres of well-tended peaches, figs, and apples. Except for this garden behind the house, the grounds were informal and natural.

Beyond the orchard to the east, a very large barn and stable contained some thirty stalls for fine blooded riding horses for the family and guests. There brood mares were carefully tended. Beyond the long row of heavily built stables and cribs were workshops, a small hamlet of whitewashed cabins, and various other outbuildings.

From the back gallery of the main house, a broad walk shaded by crepe myrtles led to the garden. Just to the left of the entrance to the garden was a strongly built masonry pen about twelve feet square with a large mound in the center, with a roofed enclosure in

[5] Strode, *Jefferson Davis: American Patriot*, p. 101.

which white rabbits were raised as pets. North of the dining room was the latticed cistern house, covered and twined with roses and honeysuckle vines.

Intersecting the crepe myrtle walk to the garden running east was a similar walk leading south to the gates of the coach house and stables. Opposite these gates stood the "Hall of Justice" where court was held for slave offenders. Beyond the stable lot spread the comfortable quarters for the plantation work forces.[6] Across the lawn in the quiet, secluded shade of an oak grove, a low, wrought-iron fence enclosed the Davis family cemetery. Samuel Davis, the patriarch of the family, was the first to be buried there.

Today, little remains at *Hurricane*. The best approach to the site is from the Louisiana side. North from Newellton, along the top of the levee past Somerset Plantation, the route leads to the ferry which crosses Palmyra Lake. On the island side, a dirt trail similar to a logging road is passable only in dry weather. It runs through flat, buckshot lowland dense with cottonwoods, indicating the old bed of the river. On a slight rise at the northernmost tip, or head, of Hurricane Island, a narrow two-mile strip in the middle of the river, grows older hardwood timber. In earlier

[6] Roach memorandum. Hudson Strode, in his *Jefferson Davis: American Patriot*, pp. 101–102, recounts many similar details which he obtained from Mrs. Mary Lucy O'Kelley, Pass Christian, Mississippi. Mrs. O'Kelley is the great granddaughter of Joseph E. Davis.

days, steamers had landed at the island to serve Davis Bend. The road crosses another buckshot bottom, formerly the chute between Hurricane Island and the mainland, and finally reaches higher, sandy ground, the original water edge of Davis Bend. Shortly, an old low levee built by Joseph Davis to protect the Bend becomes clearly discernible through the woods. Not far to the southeast, a clearing reveals the former site of the mansion. Although three big live oaks seem to have been part of a row, it is now difficult to discern any planned arrangement of trees. A rough, unpainted cabin sits on high pillars projected upon the base of the old "Greek temple structure in the garden," sometimes referred to as the library and sometimes as the bachelor quarters. On the ground underneath the cabin and all around in the tall grass are remnants of the original brick floor of the big house and its adjacent buildings. Nearby a dank, dark cistern mysteriously withholds its secrets, reflecting only distorted images in its murky mirror and mocking with eerie echoes from its hollow depths. Not far away, two more huge cisterns protrude openings near ground level. In the jumbled brick remains of a so-called commissary lie two large, rusted hulks of iron safes apparently once located in Joseph Davis' office or adjoining storeroom.

Just beyond the clearing, in the edge of the wildwood a quarter of a mile from the house site, a flattened and twisted iron fence partially encloses the sadly dilapidated burial plot guarded by one lone over-spreading oak. Tombstones leaning broken and fallen are covered by weeds and thick vines, and the brick vaults and copings have crumbled badly. Governor Dennis Murphree of Mississippi once found a large moccasin under a fallen slab, and in a marble corner near a tomb, eight new puppies had been carefully bedded by an anxious mother bristling with concern.

Most of the gravestone inscriptions are now illegible from weathering or breakage. In the midst of the plot, however, stands a large tilting shaft on a heavy square base. On one side are these words:

IN MEMORY OF
OUR GRANDFATHER
JOSEPH EMORY DAVIS
BORN DECEMBER 10, 1784
DIED SEPTEMBER 18, 1870
HE WAS JUST AND GENEROUS TO THE SORROWFUL, A
GENTLE AND SYMPATHIZING FRIEND TO THE POOR, EVER
KIND AND CHARITABLE. BLESSED ARE THE MEEK FOR
THEY SHALL INHERIT THE EARTH

On another side is carved:

ELIZA V. DAVIS
Born June 23, 1811
Died Octobr 24, 1864

Eliza, wife of Joseph, died at Lauderdale Springs

near Meridian, Mississippi where the family had sought safety following the fall of Vicksburg and possession of Davis Bend by the Federal troops. She died in 1863, not in 1864 as incorrectly recorded on the monument.

A memorial to Joseph Davis' youngest daughter, Mary, who died during a trip to Cuba, states:

IN MEMORY OF
MARY LUCINDA DAVIS
WIFE OF
CHARLES J. MITCHELL
BORN MAY 1, 1816
DIED NOVEMBER 22, 1846.

A large flat slab shows the following inscriptions:

JANE DAVIS NICHOLSON
DIED
FEBRUARY 5, 1845
AGE 27
ANDERSON DAVIS NICHOLSON
DIED
FEBRUARY 3, 1846
AGE 30 YEARS

Joe Nicholson, said to be a nephew of Eliza, was present with Joseph and Eliza when she died at Lauderdale Springs. Joe Nicholson was probably a son of Anderson and Jane Nicholson, thus the *Davis* in each name is interesting. After the war, Joe Nicholson acted as a kind of private secretary to Joseph E. Davis, to whom he referred as "Grandfather."

Another grave in the family burial plot has a stone marked:

DAVID BRADFORD
BORN
FEBRARY 2, 1796
DIED
MARCH 12, 1844.

David Bradford was the lawyer-husband of Amanda, sister of Joseph and Jefferson Davis. Judge Bradford was ambushed and assassinated by an enraged litigant as he left the courthouse in Washington, Mississippi. After his death Amanda and their seven children lived at *Hurricane.*

Another tomb bears the identification ROBBINS.[7] Other names are not clear. Caroline, Joseph's second daughter, had married Thomas E. Robins, a well-known Vicksburg banker and duelist. In 1856, after Robins had died, she married Abram F. Leonard of Norfolk, Virginia. Others rest in this family plot, but the lettering on the markers is almost impossible to decipher.

Floods, remoteness, and a lack of attention to the cemetery caused Governor Dennis Murphree in 1940 to remove the earthly dust of Samuel Davis, father of

---

[7] The correct spelling is Robins. Details of one of Robins' dueling exploits are given by Monroe F. Cockrell, *After Sundown.*

Joseph and Jefferson, to *Beauvoir* on the Gulf Coast, where his grave in the Confederate Veterans' Cemetery, on the grounds of the last home of Jefferson Davis, could be tended with respectful care. The governor, accompanied by his daughter, Mrs. Mary Frances Murphree Ford; a minister; and several friends, personally supervised the removal.

Landed neighbors just across the river from the Davises on the Louisiana side included John Perkins, a member of Congress; the O'Kelleys, one of whom— John G. O'Kelley—married Mary Lucinda Hamer, great-granddaughter of Joseph Davis; and Mrs. Sarah Dorsey of Elkton Plantation, who also owned *Beauvoir* and befriended Jefferson Davis in his declining years. Adjoining the farms of these friends stood the old Bowie home, where Jim Bowie of Alamo fame and his brother Resin lived as boys.

The big mansion at *Hurricane* is beyond the memory of living persons. On June 24, 1862, Union soldiers advancing toward Vicksburg landed on Davis Bend at night and burned *Hurricane* to the ground. Joseph E. Davis complained that General Peter J. Osterhaus ordered the burning and gave the family only thirty minutes' notice to vacate the house.[8] The red glare from the rocketing flames at the western end of the Bend could be seen in Vicksburg, eighteen direct

[8] On March 1, 1866, Joseph E. Davis wrote to President Andrew Johnson from Vicksburg, Mississippi, making application

miles away. The soldiers piled library books on the lawn and lit bonfires. They dumped sets of china and crystal on the grass and gleefully shattered them with muskets. Paintings cherished by the Davises were gathered and slashed with bayonets.

Strangely, the garden cottage detached from the house was spared. In later years, Joseph Davis' granddaughter, Mary Elizabeth (Lize) Hamer, and her family lived in this attractive little colonnaded building which was also called *Hurricane*. As a result, many persons have mistakenly believed the little garden house, last of Joseph Davis' vast *Hurricane* complex to survive, to be the original mansion. The cottage burned in 1913 and only the brick bases for its square Doric columns and irregular herringbone areas of the red brick floor remain. The deteriorated fireplaces of the central chimney all show in the dust underneath the dingy, frame shanty now propped irreverently on top of the classic foundations.

---

for the restoration of his property: "I took no part in the war. I did not bear arms. I was not a member of the legislature nor of the convention nor attended any public meetings. I contributed nothing, subscribed nothing, made no investments in Confederate bonds or securities.

Under the assurances that those would not be molested who staid [*sic*] quietly at home, I remained at my place until almost all of my property was carried off, my cotton burned and an order was received from Gen'l Osterhaus to burn my house, giving me and my family half an hour to get out. . . ." The original letter is in the possession of Judge Ben A. Guider, Vicksburg, Mississippi.

CHAPTER III

First Brierfield, *Born Out of Tragedy*

JEFFERSON, youngest of all the Davis clan, first visited Davis Bend shortly after he was graduated from the United States Military Academy at West Point in June, 1828. During that visit he met Eliza, his brother Joseph's young bride. Joseph, the senior Davis child and almost twenty-four years older than Jefferson, had assumed leadership of the family when their father, Samuel, died. Joseph had been like a father to Jefferson and had encouraged the younger boy to choose the military career upon which he was now ready to embark. During these few days together, as the brothers rode over the vast undeveloped acreage, it was not hard for them to envision the potential within this expanse of fertile land.

Soon the straight, young soldier headed for duty in the wild "Northwest" where a few settlers and many Indians vied for the same land. For seven years Lieutenant Davis grappled with frontier problems, matching his resourcefulness against primitive circumstances in the area later to become the state of Wisconsin. On one mission he contracted pneumonia as the result of severe exposure. From the gleaming snow and cold he developed a painful neuritis of the face and one eye. Although he was strong, he never fully recovered from the damage; and in later years whenever he became exhausted, he suffered great pain and swelling in the afflicted eye, which he eventually lost.

Jefferson Davis earned a good record and was highly praised by his superiors for his professional proficiency. He was also a lively and intelligent social favorite. Nevertheless, for an active young soldier, this period of routine internal national development must have seemed dull. The challenges of the service were limited, opportunities for positions of considerable responsibility were infrequent, and promotion was slow. The trivia of military regulations could, therefore, be unduly magnified by minor martinets into major incidents. In one instance Davis vigorously and successfully defended himself in a formal hearing.

During his tour of duty in the northwest the handsome lieutenant had fallen deeply in love with Sarah Knox Taylor, the appealing and attractive daughter of his commanding officer, Colonel Zachary Taylor. Because he had nearly lost his own wife to the hardships she had encourtered in remote outposts and because two of their girls had died of fever, the tough old colonel strongly and adamantly opposed his daughter's marriage to a soldier. In addition, Taylor was very cool toward Jefferson because the younger man had abruptly disagreed with him on a delicate point of army court procedure. Despite the earnest efforts of Sarah, her suitor, and their friends, Zachary Taylor could not be reconciled to the match.

In March, 1835, when all these matters came to a head at once, Jefferson decided to take a short furlough, return to *Hurricane*, and talk the situation over with Joseph. The older brother was sympathetic and helpful. Since he needed Jefferson's assistance and companionship, they decided that Jefferson should give up the army, marry Sarah, and become a planter. Joseph agreed to set aside for him ample acreage and provide the money for slaves so that Jefferson could start on his own. Although Joseph would help, Jefferson would work to clear the land and learn the problems of a large plantation just as Joseph had done.

When Jefferson returned to the Northwest, he and Sarah determined to marry immediately. In the hope of lessening the colonel's objections, Jefferson resigned his commission. He and Sarah met at Louisville, Kentucky, and were married June 17, 1835, before their friends and many members of her family at the home of her aunt near Louisville. Zachary Taylor, though still disapproving of the marriage, provided Sarah with a liberal trousseau.

Happily and bravely, the young couple launched

their honeymoon aboard a gaily bedecked steamboat bound on a leisurely journey down the Ohio and Mississippi rivers to their future home at Davis Bend. There was jubilation when the bride and groom reached *Hurricane,* and the great house reflected the genuinely warm welcome of their family. The world was fresh, green, and abundant—late June in the Deep South. Soon they were comfortably established at *Hurricane,* where they would stay until Jefferson could build a home on his farm.

Sarah's young husband was eager to begin a new career. Joseph showed Jefferson the land which was to be his own. Roughly, the part set aside to Jefferson extended from a point on the river bank near the southern tip of Hurricane Island, northeast on a diagonal line to the west end of Long Lake in the middle of the peninsula, then easterly along the south bank of the lake to the land in the eastern part of the Bend sold by Joseph to General John A. Quitman, and finally due south along the east line of Sections 18 and 23 to the river, which bounded the tract on the south.

The well-situated property afforded about two and one-half miles of river frontage; some parts were heavily wooded, while brambles covered the many ridges suitable for eventual cultivation. Uncleared land of this nature could be bought from the government at $1.25 an acre. Until improved, it had little value. Undoubtedly, the brothers had a definite understanding about the property lines, because Jefferson fenced his acreage a few years later. In fact, the Supreme Court of Mississippi confirmed that the properties were separated "by boundaries distinctly marked and frequently pointed out by the two brothers to various persons." [1]

The exact acreage was then of little moment, for there was plenty of space for both families. Jefferson thought he owned about 890 acres in Sections 18 and 23; but when the land was finally surveyed years later, according to the dividing line originally established by the Davis brothers, it was revealed to contain considerably more than the two sections. Actually included were fractional parts of four other sections, making the true acreage in Jefferson's part somewhat more than 2,320 acres. Substantial accretions along the river gradually added more acreage. Joseph retained in *Hurricane* a plantation of more than 2,960 acres, an estimate probably considerably lower than the actual extent of his holdings.

William Stamps, brother-in-law of Joseph and Jefferson as a result of his marriage to their sister Lucinda, explained that the gift of *Brierfield* to Jefferson was not altogether from Joseph. He deposed: "To my knowledge, Joseph E. Davis, in 1835, was indebted to his brother Jefferson for his part of his interest in his father's estate; because Joseph E. had all of their fath-

[1] Davis v. Bomar, 44 Mississippi Supreme Court Reports, p. 768.

er's negroes, and owed their father a considerable amount for lands he [their father] had sold him." [2] Joseph had acted as a kind of trustee for Jefferson's interest in their father's modest estate. Jefferson had actually received only James Pemberton, although he had an undivided interest in several other slaves that Joseph kept and used.

Sarah promptly accompanied Jefferson to see their new estate. In spite of the fact that it was completely untamed and was covered with undisciplined growth, it was theirs to possess proudly. Laughingly and accurately, they referred to it as "the Brierfield." The name stuck, and *Brierfield* it became. [3]

[2] *Ibid.*, p. 688.

[3] A question is often raised concerned the spelling of the name *Brierfield*, home of Jefferson Davis. Occasionally the word is written *Briarfield* rather than *Brierfield*. Either *brier* or *briar* may refer to a bramble or thorny bush a prickly plant or shrub. The most common spelling, especially during the early part of the nineteenth century, has been *brier*. Variant spellings occur in Jefferson Davis' *The Rise and Fall of the Confederate Government* and in Varina Howell Davis' *Jefferson Davis, Ex-President of the Confederate States, A Memoir by His Wife*. In *The Rise and Fall of the Confederate Government*, the caption to a drawing of the home and an entry in the list of illustrations are printed *Briarfield*. Yet throughout the text, and when the name is given as an originating address of correspondence, the spelling is *Brierfield*. Likewise, the first large volume of Mrs. Davis' *Memoir* is sprinkled with the *er* spelling, although a sketch of the house is labeled *Briarfield*. Early references in the second volume use the *ar* spelling, but toward the end of the volume the *er* spelling occurs rather consistently. Apparently, the confusion has been perpetuated by transcription of dictation or by the publishers' use of illustrations carrying the *ar* spelling. Nevertheless, the original correspondence of Mr. and Mrs.

Before any substantial clearing was undertaken, the brothers, accompanied by James Pemberton, Jefferson's faithful and trusted servant and foreman, journeyed to Natchez to secure laborers for the formidable task ahead. They selected twenty slaves from those offered for sale. Although Joseph did the negotiating and attended to the financial arrangements, everyone distinctly understood that Jefferson Davis was the purchaser and master. The men returned to the Bend with twenty new slaves to begin the laborious clearing of *Brierfield*. Occasionally, some of the slaves from *Hurricane* came over to help. James Pemberton was in charge of the operation.

In mid-August, 1835, Jefferson contracted malaria from the mosquitoes that infested the swamps and woods during the summer. The day after Jefferson became ill, the delicate Sarah Knox came down with chills and fever. In an effort to avoid effects of the sickness, they decided to visit Jefferson's sister Anna, Mrs. Luther Smith, near St. Francisville, Louisiana. Both became dangerously ill after they arrived at Anna's home, *Locust Grove* on Bayou Sara. On September 15, 1835, the beloved and fragile Sarah, a bride of three months, died in her husband's arms and was bur-

---

Davis, as well as other family papers, refers to *Brierfield*. Most conclusively, however, the land records and court documents relied on during the long and tedious litigation involving the property recorded the name as *Brierfield*. Without any doubt, Jefferson Davis named and referred to his home as *Brierfield*.

ied at *Locust Grove*. He, too, was desperately ill. Following this heartbreak, Davis had neither the desire nor the strength to continue the work at *Brierfield*. During a period of aimless travel and recuperation, he was attended by James Pemberton, his dependable companion of army days in the frontier Northwest. Eventually, the grieving Jefferson returned to take up the task he had temporarily abandoned. Hard, sweating, bone-breaking work provided therapy for an aching heart. As *Brierfield* yielded to his fierce demands, his spirit mended.

After the crop was harvested in late 1838, Jefferson and James Pemberton constructed the first owner's residence at *Brierfield*. Many years later, in her memoir, Varina Davis recalled that about six weeks after she and Jefferson were married, they lived in a " 'cat and clayed' house, situated in the centre of, and behind, a magnificent grove of oaks, and flanked by thrifty fig trees; the Quarter houses being to the right and left of us." She continued:

> The building was one of my hubsand's experiments as an architect, and he and his friend and servant, James Pemberton, built it with the help of the negroes on the plantation. The rooms were of fair size, and opened on a paved brick gallery, surrounded by latticework; but some miscalculation about the windows had placed the sills almost breast high. The outer doors were six feet wide, but on these he especially

dwelt as most desirable for admitting plenty of cool air; however, when they were opened, the side of the house seemed to be taken down. The fireplaces were very deep, and looked as though they had been built in Queen Elizabeth's time, to roast a sheep whole. It was a cool house, comfortably furnished. . . .[4]

Through "blood, sweat and tears," Jefferson began to achieve a measure of the good life at *Brierfield*.

[4] Varina Howell Davis, *Jefferson Davis, Ex-President*, I, 202–203.

BRIERFIELD TODAY

Front view from south side. Original pillars (behind oak tree) are overgrown with vines.

Rear view from north. Growth beyond cistern covers the remains.

Rear view looking west. House pillars are at left. Hunting lodge in distance under trees is recent structure.

Chimney and fireplace near center of ruins.

Photographs by William G. Beanland

GARDEN COTTAGE AT HURRICANE, 1865–1900

Main house, which burned in 1862, was located behind trees at left. This cottage burned in 1919.

HURRICANE GARDEN COTTAGE, ABOUT 1865

Sometimes called the library, this building was spared in 1862 when Union soldiers destroyed the main house. The building is sometimes erroneously referred to as the original hurricane mansion. The Negroes standing before the house were probably slaves of Joseph Davis. In later years members of the Joseph E. Davis family lived here.

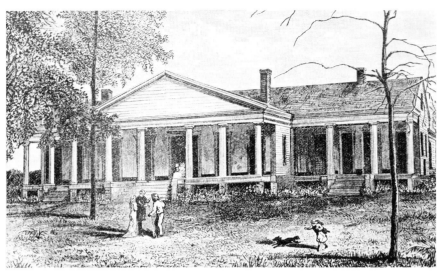

BRIERFIELD

This drawing was first published in 1881 in Jefferson Davis' *Rise and Fall of the Confederate Government.* In Mrs. Varina Davis' memoir of her husband, published in 1890, the drawing appeared with the figures omitted and a horse and buggy replacing the girl and dog at lower right.

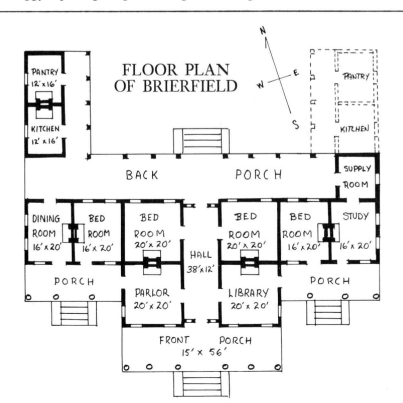

FLOOR PLAN OF BRIERFIELD

PANTRY 12' x 16'

KITCHEN 12' x 16'

PANTRY

KITCHEN

BACK PORCH

SUPPLY ROOM

DINING ROOM 16' x 20'

BED ROOM 16' x 20'

BED ROOM 20' x 20'

BED ROOM 20' x 20'

BED ROOM 16' x 20'

STUDY 16' x 20'

HALL 38' x 12'

PORCH

PARLOR 20' x 20'

LIBRARY 20' x 20'

PORCH

FRONT PORCH 15' x 56'

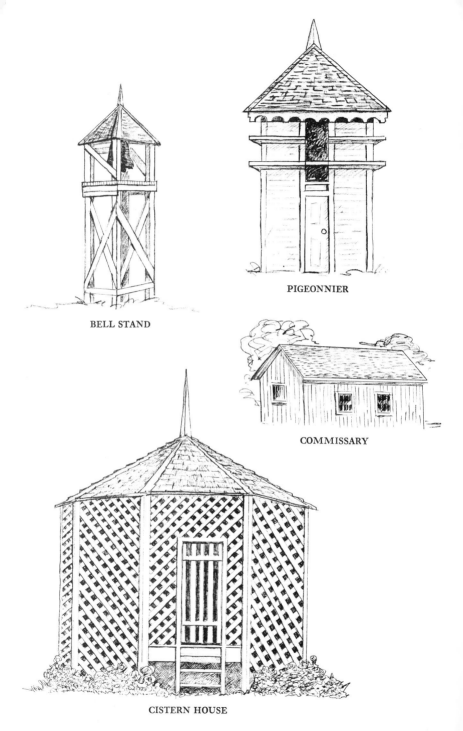

BELL STAND

PIGEONNIER

COMMISSARY

CISTERN HOUSE

These structures, all originally located on the grounds of Brierfield, were sketched by the author from photographs lent by Mrs. Henry Bobb of Vicksburg, Mississippi.

A. B. Ward, from Harper's Weekly, *September 15, 1866*

NEGRO QUARTERS AT BRIERFIELD

Jefferson Hayes-Davis, Colorado Springs, Colorado

BRIERFIELD GIN AND SHEDS

Blanks Studio, Vicksburg | Miss Clara Stevens, Yokena, Mississippi

BRIERFIELD, 1890–1910

Commissary and part of bell stand at extreme right. Pigeonnier partially visible behind house at left. Screen on front porch, latticework, and fences near house were added during this period.

BRIERFIELD IN FLOOD OF 1920

The water did not rise as high as in 1922 (see illustration below). Repeated floods led Jefferson Hayes-Davis to raise the house on high pillars.

BRIERFIELD: HIGH WATER, 1922

BRIERFIELD, 1924
Front entrance shortly after house was elevated to avoid floodwaters.

BRIERFIELD, 1924
Only known photograph showing back of house.

BRIERFIELD, 1931

Photograph by former Governor Dennis Murphree. This is probably the last photograph of Brierfield. It was published in the Memphis *Commercial Appeal* on Sunday, April 5, 1931, two weeks after the house burned.

CHAPTER IV

"The Best Laid Schemes . . ."

BY THE TIME *Brierfield* had achieved recognition as a producing plantation, the youth who had initiated its transformation had become a man seasoned in body and mind. A new day dawned and a new man emerged.

On February 26, 1845, Jefferson Davis was married to lovely Varina Howell in Natchez. He was thirty-seven years old and she only nineteen. They moved into the cottage at *Brierfield*. The next few months of spring, summer, and autumn were idyllic. Varina fondly reminisced:

> We passed many happy days there, enlivened by daily rides, in which we indulged in many races when the road was smooth. The game was more abundant then than chickens are now. Wild geese in great flocks, made fat by the waste corn in the fields; wild ducks by the thousand, and white and blue cranes adorned almost every slough, standing on one leg among the immense lily-pads that . . . cover the low

places with lemon-colored flowers as large as coffee-cups.[1]

Public issues of the day, however, lured the planter away from total dedication to the soil. Jefferson's interest in politics became stronger, and late in 1845 he was elected to Congress as a Democrat. Early in December, he and Varina arrived in Washington, D. C., to assume their role in the nation's public affairs. Within six months, however, the United States was at war with Mexico. Fighting loomed. Jefferson Davis felt that he must volunteer. Varina, possessive and perhaps insecure, opposed his going. Although she pleaded, argued, struggled, and cried, Jefferson once again committed himself to military service.

With excitement and much eagerness, Jefferson left Congress to accept command of the Mississippi Regiment that had chosen him as its colonel. But he was apprehensive regarding Varina, whose deep moods and variable temperament posed problems. Enroute to Vicksburg by steamboat on July 8, 1846, Jefferson wrote confidingly to his dear sister Lucinda that Varina was not well and had refused to stay in the North where he wished her to spend the summer. Almost pathetically, he commented:

> If circumstances warranted it I would send her to you. To you and your family alone of all the world

[1] Varina Howell Davis, *Jefferson Davis, Ex-President*, I, 203.

could I entrust her and rest assured that no wayward-
ness would ever lessen kindness. . . . She will probably stay with her mother most of the time during
which I will be absent. With Eliza [Joseph's semi-
invalid wife] she could not be contented, nor would
their residing together increase their good feeling for
each other. This distresses me as you will readily
imagine, but if you ever have an opportunity to un-
derstand Varina's character, you will see the pro-
priety of the conclusion, and I feel that you will love
her too much to take heed of the weaknesses which
spring from a sensitive and generous temper. . . .[2]

Miserable, bitter, and disappointed to the point of
sickness, yet loving Jefferson above all, Varina declared to her mother that during his absence "no earthly power shall persuade me to live with anyone else
but you." [3]

At *Hurricane*, Jefferson left his resignation from
Congress for Joseph to forward to Washington. He
hastened to New Orleans to catch up with his regiment which was to leave for Mexico on July 26, 1846.
Upon his arrival at Brazos Island, Colonel Davis received a very cordial and friendly letter from General Zachary Taylor, indicating that any past differ-
ences between them had been forgotten. The recon-
ciliation was complete.

[2] Hudson Strode, *Jefferson Davis: Private Letters 1823–1889*
(New York: Harcourt, Brace & World, Inc., 1966), p. 40.
[3] *Ibid.*, p. 39.

Jefferson put his men through a very severe training period that caused some grumbling, but in six weeks they participated in hard fighting which resulted in the capture of Monterrey on September 24, 1846. Joseph was glad that his brother had escaped harm; but always dominant and imperious in attitude, he strongly deplored the failure of the Americans to compel an unconditional surrender instead of allowing the Mexicans to march out with honors of war. Since he expected a short war, Joseph withheld Jefferson's resignation from Congress.

In October, 1846, James Pemberton reported from *Brierfield* that he had picked 170,000 pounds of cotton and would make over 300 bales—almost as much as the *Hurricane* crop. All was going well on the farm. *Brierfield* had become an exceptionally productive plantation unit, virtually on a par with Joseph's great *Hurricane* place in spite of less acreage. Jefferson was achieving both fame and independence.

At this point, Varina's erratic temperament and her uncertainty about herself involved her in an open controversy with the Davis family. She related the incident as follows:

> The year after my marriage, and while my husband was in Mexico, I was wounded by remarks made in the family, alleging my husband's dependence upon his brother, and went to Mr. Joseph E. Davis to put to him the direct question, "Is my hus-

band the owner of Brierfield, or is he dependent upon you? Do you or does he own Brierfield?" To which Mr. Joseph E. Davis responded that he had given my husband the land, and assisted him in the beginning of its settlement, and that I must not mind such ill-natured and wild remarks as led to my inquiry; that my husband stood in the place of a son to him.[4]

Varina was possessive and headstrong. Joseph was possessive and headstrong. Each was unwilling to surrender any claim upon Jefferson. Varina vehemently considered Joseph hostile to her and directly accused him of such an attitude, which he always strongly denied. Nevertheless, trouble developed. Varina became so upset that she urged Jefferson to return home because of her illness. In the midst of the war, Colonel Davis obtained a sixty-day emergency leave and rushed back to Mississippi in October, 1846, only to find Varina surprisingly well but emotionally overwrought. He tried his best to straighten matters and smooth ruffled feelings. On the surface at least, peace was restored.

With Joseph's legal help, Jefferson wrote his will. He also made arrangements for Varina to stay at *Brierfield Cottage* rather than with her mother in Natchez or with the Davis family at *Hurricane*. Mary Jane (Malie) Bradford, twenty-two—the same age as Varina—agreed to spend the nights with Varina at

[4] Davis v. Bomar, 55 Mississippi Reports, p. 702.

Brierfield. Malie, the daughter of Amanda, had lived with her uncle and Varina in Washington during the time Jefferson was in Congress; and she and Varina were congenial. While he was at home on this furlough, Jefferson decided to build a new house for Varina at *Brierfield,* and they discussed this important project. In early December, the colonel returned to the war in Mexico.

Brooding and sullen, the young Varina—comparable in spirit to Scarlett O'Hara, the fictional heroine of Margaret Mitchell's *Gone With the Wind*—was determined by her very presence at *Brierfield* to establish beyond question its independence. With James Pemberton, she would attend to the operations without assistance from Brother Joseph. Preferring to be alone during the day, yet resentfully so, she plunged into housework, laying carpets, arranging furniture, cooking, and "projecting immense improvements." [5] She filled her days with an almost primitive intensity of effort. She confessed; "I have become quite a savage, I declare, I feel better alone than with anyone, though my own plate looks very lonely, and I tear my food in silence." [6]

Varina went to *Hurricane* as seldom as possible, but the Davises, including Brother Joseph, came often to see her at *Brierfield.* She dreaded to see the Bradford

[5] Strode, *Jefferson Davis: Private Letters*, p. 46.
[6] *Ibid.*, p. 45.

gang of small children coming because they were very unruly and destructive. She complained that they cluttered her clean carpets with food "thrown from one side of the room to the other." [7] On January 5, 1847, the busy, but lonely, mistress of *Brierfield* wrote, "In a few weeks I intend setting the negroes to brick making, and do hope I may be able to make brick enough before Jeff comes home to make the house he wants me to build." [8]

Jefferson Davis returned from Mexico in June, 1847, a national hero on account of his brilliant performance at Buena Vista. For two years he found it necessary to use crutches because of a wound received when he was shot through the foot. Though weak and worn, he was home at last and Varina was happy. Now they could proceed with their plans to build a home worthy of a man of national prominence and stature.

About this time, a very difficult problem arose concerning the proposed new residence. Joseph probably introduced the idea, but Jefferson seemed to accept it favorably. Since Jefferson had become a public figure, heavy demands upon his time from the outside would make it necessary for him to be away from *Brierfield* frequently. Thus Varina would be alone quite often. At the same time, Amanda Bradford and her children

[7] *Ibid.*
[8] *Ibid.*, p. 46.

needed more room than they enjoyed at *Hurricane*, which was crowded in spite of its considerable size. Why not build *Brierfield* so that Jefferson and Varina could live in one part and the Bradfords in another? The house could be planned to have separate living quarters and even two kitchens, but at the same time Amanda could provide company for Varina. Although both men rather liked the idea, Varina did not; and Jefferson was caught in the middle. In midsummer, Varina confided to her mother:

> This miserable business of Brother Joe's has given him [Jefferson] more pain if possible than I expected, however, I have determined to preserve perfect silence upon the subject until we can talk about it without it exciting either of us. The family and myself are upon as good terms as usual. I do not go there oftener than I can help, and they come down [to Brierfield] almost every day to see Jeff, and treat me with respect. My good sister Amanda and the girls come when they can, and I feel always glad to see them.[9]

Meanwhile, Varina continued landscaping the grounds that would surround the house whenever it was built. She set out a great many trees, including a number of cedars and pines, and planted decorative vines which grew well and added beauty to her plans. Varina hoped that if she continued to be an industri-

[9] *Ibid.*, p. 48.

ous wife and kept wisely quiet, "all will be happy yet."[10]

In the midst of this situation, Governor Albert Gallatin Brown on August 10, 1847, appointed Jefferson United States senator to fill the vacancy created by the death of Senator Jesse Speight.[11] The whole family was elated over Jefferson's appointment, and house plans were temporarily submerged in other activity. Jefferson's enforced absence would, however, add plausibility to the plan for sharing the occupancy of *Brierfield*. Early in November, 1847, Jefferson had a number of long, last minute business conferences with Joseph and then departed for Washington, leaving Varina behind for the time being. On December 6, 1847, the oath as Senator was administered to Jefferson Davis, who was still on crutches.

All was apparently congenial at *Hurricane* and at *Brierfield*, which was now a thriving plantation with a steam cotton gin, quarters, and other buildings. In January, 1848, however, when the question of sharing the house was again mentioned, Varina, with some pique and sarcasm, confided to her mother:

> Everyone is affectionate—some decision has been arrived at about the house, but as I am so little concerned it has not been thought proper to inform me. I always speak as if it were mine, and no one else's,

[10] *Ibid.*
[11] Strode, *Jefferson Davis: American Patriot*, p. 190.

so I suppose all will be straight. The subject is never mentioned. They are as affectionate as they can be, and in trying to do my whole duty, I am happy, and absolutely look upon Jeff's displeasure or pleasure as a minor consideration to my own duty. . . .[12]

Unquestionably, Jefferson had stepped in and assumed firm control of the home-building problem. Varina, no doubt, felt that Joseph was at the bottom of her trouble, and Joseph, in turn, considered that Varina was pushing too ambitiously.

The Mississippi Supreme Court in 1878 found that "the plan [for dual occupancy] did not originate with Joseph E.," [13] but Varina thought it did. Nevertheless, Jefferson had decided that the best way to provide companionship and protection for Varina during his many absences and at the same time fulfill his duty toward his widowed sister, Amanda Bradford, was to build a house that could be shared by both families.

Sometime in 1848, either in January or after he returned home from the Senate adjournment in July, Jefferson Davis negotiated a contract to build a new house. Mrs. Davis related the circumstances as follows:

In the years 1847 and 1848, Mr. Davis on account of his sister, Mrs. Bradford, not being content at "Hurricane," and because my health did not permit

[12] Strode, *Jefferson Davis: Private Letters*, pp. 56–57.
[13] Davis v. Bomar, 55 Mississippi Reports, p. 773.

me to travel to and from Washington, determined to plan a house large enough for his sister to live in one end and we in the other. He made a contract with Messrs. Marcy & Zeigler for a ten-thousand dollar house, the heavy timbers to be cut on our own swamp land. A part, if not all of the frame-work came from Cincinnati and Vicksburg, I believe. This contract covered all except the filling up of the library and the purchase of marble mantel-pieces for the house. Mr. Davis paid for the house by drafts upon his commission merchants, Messrs. Laughlin & Co. . . .[14]

The contract was made with Jefferson Davis, and the house and outhouses were built under his direction in spite of the fact that he was absent from home during a considerable part of 1848. W. H. Zeigler, who was only fourteen years old in 1848 and an apprentice carpenter, recalled that "it was rather a costly residence . . . either $5,000 or $6,000." [15] Zeigler's knowledge about the price and the contract must have been primarily hearsay—what he was told.

David Lanmaster, in 1848 a journeyman carpenter for Marcy and Zeigler and later a partner, recalled that his firm contracted "for the carpenter's work and materials, plastering, painting, glazing, and everything else except the frame timber, and that was cut on the place." [16] He assisted Zeigler, Marcy, his brother Wil-

[14] *Ibid.*, p. 693.
[15] *Ibid.*, p. 692.
[16] *Ibid.*, p. 696.

liam Lanmaster, and Lewis Jones in building the dwelling house and some of the outhouses. Lanmaster affirmed that "there were two kitchens put to the house, for the reason that it was intended to be occupied by two families." [17]

So work on the new *Brierfield* proceeded. Varina was on hand most of the time, although Jefferson was away very frequently. Joseph kept an eye on the construction, but he was not too pleased with the project. He grumbled to his daughter, Mrs. Florida Laughlin, who recalled: "My father said the erection of the house on Brierfield was an absurd extravagance on my uncle's part, because of his staying there so little. Mr. and Mrs. Jefferson Davis planned the house." [18]

Varina personally supervised many of the details in construction. On one occasion, in the absence of her husband, she insisted on a change in kitchen plans. When Joseph objected to the additional cost, Varina tartly told him that if this were *his* kitchen she would not insist, but since it was *her* kitchen, she would have it as she wished.

William Stamps, with some assurance and deliberation, asserted that "he [Jefferson Davis] built and occupied his house as early as 1850, at least, after his return from Mexico." [19] Mrs. Davis declared that "the

[17] *Ibid.*, p. 697.
[18] *Ibid.*, p. 694.
[19] *Ibid.*, p. 690.

house was finished in 1849 or 1850." [20] At another time, she recalled that they moved into the new house "five years after her marriage" in 1845. [21] The house itself was probably finished during 1849 or 1850, as Varina has indicated, but quite likely the entire plantation improvement project, including gin, dependencies, fences, quarters, and other work, was not concluded until 1852. Subsequently, even further improvements were effected at *Brierfield*, and some of the carpenters stayed on the place until 1855. [22]

At any rate, the new structure was never to house two families. Varina explained: "Mrs. Bradford and I mutually declined to live together, neither of us being willing to be subordinate in household jurisdiction, which resulted in Mr. Davis and my taking possession of our house alone." [23] "The best laid schemes o' mice and men gang aft a-gley," particularly when unyielding female wills are involved.

[20] *Ibid.,* p. 693.
[21] Varina Howell Davis, *Jefferson Davis, Ex-President,* I, 204.
[22] Davis v. Bomar, 55 Mississippi Reports, p. 697.
[23] *Ibid.,* pp. 693–694.

CHAPTER V

Home for a Planter-Statesman

ALL OF DAVIS BEND was flat—very flat. No hills, mounds, or bluffs rose above the even alluvial plain, gradually corrugated with shallow swales and barely perceptible ridges. At the edge of the river, the level land dropped straight down an eroded bank about thirty feet to the normal water stage. The house at *Brierfield* was located in a natural park of large oak and wild pecan trees, almost in the exact center of Jefferson's tract, a mile and three-fourths southeast of Joseph Davis' mansion at *Hurricane*. *Brierfield* faced southwest and was set back a mile and a quarter from the river on one of the higher undulations of the compact sandy-loam land. Because of the distance and the tall, thick intervening trees, the river could not be seen from the house.

Without professional architectural guidance, Jefferson Davis and his wife planned a house to reflect their own characters. The architecture expressed classic, disciplined simplicity—a clean, naked, unadorned honesty of design and purpose. The house seemed to grow out of the ground that supported it—solid, strong, and deeply rooted. Without the least hint of ostentation, the structure quietly evinced independence of mind, modest assurance, and elegant contentment. Remotely situated almost at the end of the road in the midst of a semi-wilderness, the home was not so much to be seen as to be lived in.

The style was dictated by the features Jefferson and Varina most wanted: plenty of space, protection from the still night dampness that supposedly brought malarial diseases, and wide ample porches to provide shaded coolness during the day. The house possessed unity as well as compartmented privacy for the versatile activities of homelife combined with the business of running a plantation and the demands of a public career.

The Davises had good reasons for choosing a spreading, one-story building instead of the majestic upright multi-storied grandness of the traditional white-pillared southern mansion. Land was abundant. In addition, Davis Bend was almost a world unto itself without many people around to impress. They may well have considered the severe damage the wind had done to the tall, massive, and exposed *Hurricane*. A house built close to the ground would probably stand a better chance of surviving the strong cyclonic winds which occasionally swept over the Bend from the southwest. Perhaps, also, they wanted to build a house different from Joseph's rambling and pretentious *Hurricane*. Certainly the temporarily crippled Mexican War veteran needed a place where he could get about on his crutches without the difficulty of stairs. They made their wishes known to Zeigler and Marcy, master builders, who constructed the dwelling to fulfill the Davises' expressed requirements for rooms and space.

The house had no known pattern or prototype. The style, adapted to the Davises' individual mode of living, was distinctive in its simplicity. In some ways, *Brierfield* suggested the upper part of *Concord* in Natchez, without its circled steps and lower floor. Then, too, the long, inviting first-floor gallery of *The Briers*, Varina's girlhood home in Natchez, may have influenced Jefferson and Varina.

The long, low, one-story house afforded pleasant relaxation and comfort. Ample porches across the front captured the prevailing southwest breezes, filtered fresh and clean through the cooling shade of numerous spreading trees. Maximum advantage was derived from nature's air conditioning. None of the bedrooms or parlors had any significant exposure to the hot sun. All the rooms were protected by deep galleries front and back, and each room either connected directly or offered easy access to a porch. The spreading house rested on brick pillars forty inches above ground to provide ventilation underneath. A heavy roof constructed of hand-hewn cypress shingles and a spacious attic provided insulation above the main floor.[1]

Because of the width of the central portico span, the pediment over the elongated architrave was heavy and dominant, with a minimum of molding or enrichment. No fanlight or decoration broke the severe triangular middle expanse supported by six fluted, Doric columns. The entrance was inviting, informal, and hospitable. The exterior of the house was painted a gleaming white and trimmed with louvered outside window blinds of cypress painted dark green. Set back slightly on both sides of the main gallery were two balanced wings, each with separate recessed porches lined with three columns matching those in the middle. This architectural device created a broken colonnade effect the entire length of the house.

The handsome doorway in the center of the front porch provided entrance into a spacious middle hall running through the house from front to back. The parlor to the immediate left and the library to the

[1] For many of the details relating to the house at *Brierfield*, I am greatly indebted to Mr. Victor Bobb, Vicksburg, Mississippi. After measuring the porches and rooms of the house and observing the details of construction, he produced a scale model of the dwelling, sketched the inside arrangements, and noted the interior decoration of the rooms. Measurements of the brick foundations that still remain confirm the accuracy of his notes and floor plan.

right were both accessible from the hall. The master bedroom was located farther back to the left, with a guest room situated across the hall on the right. Each of these central rooms off the hall measured twenty feet square.

The east wing, accessible from the side porch adjoining the library, consisted of a smaller bedroom and a study at the end. The west wing contained another bedroom and the dining room on the west end, both accessible from the front and back porches. All rooms in these wings measured sixteen by twenty feet.

A brick kitchen and pantry projected northward perpendicular to the west wing of the house and the dining room. A service porch connected these facilities with the back porch. A similar kitchen arrangement originally constructed for the east wing was apparently removed sometime after the Civil War, and the east end of the back porch was enclosed for a supply, or storage, room. The kitchen and pantry were each twelve by sixteen feet.

The front porch was fifteen feet deep and fifty-six feet long, while the side porches measured twelve feet wide and thirty-four feet long. A long back porch fifteen feet wide and one hundred twenty-four feet long extended the entire length of the house.

Steam planing mills in Cincinnati probably supplied such important millwork as columns, doors, windows, and door and window frames. Other framing came

from Vicksburg, while the heavier foundation timbers were cut from trees on the plantation. The eight
by eight inch rough hewn cypress sills rested on brick
foundation pillars. The floor joists were two and one-
half by eight inch cypress placed two feet apart, a
somewhat wider than usual spacing. Floors throughout the house were made of one by six inch red cypress
fitted boards.

The proportions for the classic Doric portico and
columns undoubtedly were correctly and meticu-
lously calculated from a practical builder's guide or
manual generally used at the time by contractors in
the South. The tapered, fluted, Doric columns were
about twelve feet high, eighteen inches in diameter at
the base and twelve inches at the top. They were not
solid but were constructed of thick cypress pieces
mitered together and held by wooden pins, then
planed round and shaped. The back porch columns
were square and straight.

All the doors were twelve feet high, and the windows on the front extended twelve feet from the floor
to provide good ventilation and light. Inside, window
and door framing was plain. There was little, if any,
molding where the walls reached the ceiling and no
medallions or ornamentation overhead. Hardware for
the doors and windows was brass. One close observer
commented that the ceilings were all eighteen feet
high and a Davis descendant remembered the ceilings

as "very high." [2] When photographs of the house are carefully scaled, however, it would appear that the ceilings were probably nearer sixteen feet high. The interior finish and decoration were simply executed. Interior walls throughout the house, as well as the exterior walls which were protected by porches, were plaster over wood lathing, and the inside walls were painted, not papered. The exposed siding was overlapping cypress board.

Concessions to ostentation were few. Mrs. Davis took great pride in two mantels made of white Cararra marble imported from Italy. These graced the parlor and library fireplaces. Two chandeliers decorated and illuminated the dining room. The large, squarely built front door was handsomely framed by three clear glass lights on each side and three larger glass panels above.

Numerous smaller buildings served the needs of the large plantation. In a line at the rear of the house, three large cisterns, latticed and shingle covered for coolness and protection, held the clean rain water used at *Brierfield*. A short distance both east and west of the Big House were two rows of slave cabins, five on each side.

Approximately sixty yards behind the house to the north, the dirt road from *Hurricane* to Vicksburg ran in a long straight stretch. About a fourth of a mile

[2] Jefferson Hayes-Davis (grandson of Jefferson Davis), letter to the author, January 12, 1966.

west of the house, on the south side of this road, stood the little steam cotton gin with adjacent sheds for equipment, seed, and bale storage. Corn cribs, a pigeoneire, and the other usual utility buildings were judiciously placed about the premises. A small commissary to supply the needs of the *Brierfield* residents was located near the gate to the east entrance to the house.

In a secluded little cemetery a short distance to the southeast of the house rested the deceased slaves of *Brierfield*, respected and honored.

The entire outer perimeter of the *Brierfield* acreage was fenced. Additional neater fences enclosed the house area—particularly along the road. Most of these inner fences were covered with running roses.

All in all, *Brierfield*, with its strongly built, elegantly simple main house and its numerous outlying buildings, met the needs of the Davises and provided them a comfortable home.

CHAPTER VI

Refuge and Refreshment

By LATE SUMMER, 1849, when Jefferson and Varina Davis returned to Davis Bend from Washington, the new house at *Brierfield* was probably nearly completed. During the autumn they very likely made preliminary plans for moving into the new home. Then they left Mississippi in time to reach the nation's capital for the opening of the Thirty-first Congress on December 3, 1849.

Senator Davis would find 1850 a busy year in Washington. In addition to his important duties as Chairman of the Committee of Military Affairs, he faced other heavy responsibilities and problems. Henry Clay's proposal for handling slavery in the new western lands created great tension. When John C. Calhoun died, Davis attended the funeral in Charleston, South Carolina, as an honor escort. Then his friend and former father-in-law, President Zachary Taylor, died in office. Congress finally adjourned in the fall of 1850.

Jefferson Davis was praised by the legislature for his faithful service and was elected to a full senatorial term of six years. As the white cotton was being picked in October, 1850, Jefferson sought rest and refuge at *Brierfield*.

Undoubtedly, this autumn when the Davises first occupied their new home must have been a happy time. At last they owned a house fit for a successful planter and distinguished senator-statesman. In this cherished place, Jefferson and Varina with some excitement enjoyed a fruitful fall, a mild winter, and a blooming early spring. In April, 1851, they traveled back to Washington. Their next visit home was to be less pleasant.

Called at the last minute by the Mississippi Democrats, Jefferson Davis resigned from the Senate to run for governor against Henry S. Foote in 1851. September found him at *Brierfield*, sick with malaria. His left eye had become inflamed and swollen and almost burst from the pressure within. Varina nursed her husband day and night in their new master bedroom which was darkened to keep out the light. Jefferson recovered enough to campaign only briefly and inadequately. He lost the November election by only 999 votes.

Having served his country to the best of his ability in both Washington and Mississippi, Jefferson Davis settled down at his new home to enjoy the life of a country squire, free for the first time in many years from any public responsibility. From November, 1851, to March, 1853, Jefferson Davis enjoyed the happiest days he would ever spend at *Brierfield*, or perhaps at any other place during his lifetime.

It was a delightful interlude. Varina was not disappointed that Jefferson had lost the election for governor. She was content at home and set about making a fall garden, writing to her parents October 28, 1851: "I have a vegetable ivory nut growing, and some beautiful plants from Chile, Brazil and Turkey, some from John Perkins (across the River), some from my kind old friend Mr. Seaton in Washington. So much verbena that I cannot get it all planted, scarlet, pink, white, lilac, royal purple and crimson." [1]

In 1852 spring came early. By March, roses were in bud and almost ready to bloom; tomatoes were already a foot and a half high. Hundreds of beet plants displayed four leaves, eggplants had six, and peppers showed eight. Jefferson was well and thoroughly satisfied with his home. Often he worked so long in the field that he was almost too tired to talk. His pleasure was marred only by the partial estrangement with his brother Joseph, which began in 1850. "Happy in the peaceful pursuits of a planter busily engaged in cares for servants, in the improvement of my land, in build-

[1] Strode, *Jefferson Davis: Private Letters,* pp. 63–64.

ing, in rearing live stock, and the like occupations," he wrote, "the time passed pleasantly away. . . ." [2]

Years later, Mrs. Davis recalled this period at *Brierfield* and wrote in her *Memoir:* "After the canvass resulted against the Democratic party, we began to put our home in order; for, on our return, after a long absence, the little woman who had charge of the house told me, with friendly sympathy, 'Missis, 'tain't no use to talk; what isn't broke is crack, and what isn't crack is broke.' " [3] After their lengthy absence, the Davises found a great deal of repair work needed to be done around the house and grounds. Varina remembered particularly Davis' desire to improve the garden. She wrote: "My husband was very fond of cultivating trees and of seeing roses and ornamental shrubs blooming about us. We worked together in the garden the greater part of the day, and whenever he thought of it he laughed over one of our two gardeners sending an order for seeds to New Orleans, with the endorsement upon the outside of the letter: 'Please send these seeds immediately, if not sooner. John O'Connor, Gardener.' The crudities of this class of people entertained him very much. . . ." [4]

During this leisurely sojourn at *Brierfield* the Davises enjoyed time for reading books, the mail which was delivered twice a week, and occasional visits from

[2] Varina Howell Davis, *Jefferson Davis, Ex-President,* I, 476.
[3] *Ibid.,* p. 474.
[4] *Ibid.*

neighbors. Varina recounted that another pleasure was the "daily ride on our fast racing horses, with races on the smooth road wherever we found one. . . . There was thirty seconds' difference in the speed of our horses, our races were rather even, and we enjoyed the exercise exceedingly. Nothing could be more pleasant than the dense shade through which we could ride for miles, in air redolent of the perfume of the moss, flowers, wild crabapple and plum blossoms." [5]

Occasionally, the routine of plantation life was broken by incidents which remained in Varina's mind as she wrote her account of these years. She never forgot the alligator hunts and described one in her memoirs.

> Sometimes a calf was missing and then my husband went to hunt the alligator that had probably taken it. Once he had a very remarkable success in punishing one that had killed two calves. The negroes found its hole, and Mr. Davis put a long cane down it until the creature seized it in its mouth. He then put the gun on a line with the cane and shot the alligator in the mouth. He was an immense animal and a post-mortem examination justified the killing, for the last calf was found in part. [6]

Regarding plant growth on the island, Varina remarked that "the land is so fertile at Brierfield and in

[5] *Ibid.*, p. 475.
[6] *Ibid.*

'the adjacent country that golden-rod grows large enough for a strong walking-stick and the heads of the bloom are like banks of gold on the sides of the road. In every slough the lotos covers the surface with its lemon-colored chalices, and the green leaves are nearly a foot across. We planted a little switch, or scion of live-oak, with an attenuated little root, in 1852, and now it shades ninety feet in all directions, and is over six feet in circumference. 'Possession crowns endeavor' there, and that quickly." [7]

To augment such domestic bliss, their first child, Samuel, was "born in the Big House" [8] at *Brierfield* in July, 1852. There was sadness, too, for Jefferson's beloved friend and servant, James Pemberton, died in 1852 and was respectfully buried in the slave cemetery a little southeast of the *Brierfield* house. James, more than any other person—probably including Jefferson—had, through his management of *Brierfield* in its early days, helped to establish it as a fine plantation. He was deeply mourned.

The quiet life was too good to last. President-elect Franklin Pierce persuaded Jefferson Davis to accept the position as Secretary of War in his Cabinet. Jefferson and Varina returned to Washington in March, 1853, as important members of the Pierce administra-

[7] *Ibid.*, pp. 475–476.
[8] Dennis Murphree, "Hurricane and Brierfield, The Plantations," *Journal of Mississippi History*, IX (April, 1947), 107.

tion. During the next four years, they would enjoy fewer journeys to the Bend, although these brief visits would be quite pleasant. The best years of *Brierfield* spanned the time from 1850 to 1857.

CHAPTER VII

Prosperity and Adversity

IN SPITE OF the master's many lengthy absences from
Brierfield, the plantation produced well; and, as a result, Jefferson's wealth was markedly increased. During the years 1853–1857, he also achieved notable
success and prominence in Washington. An active,
energetic, and resourceful Secretary of War, he had
also become President Pierce's chief confidant; and
when his cabinet term ended on March 4, 1857, Davis
was immediately sworn in as Senator from Mississippi.

In early May, after Congress had recessed for the
summer, Jefferson and Varina left with their family
and entourage for a vacation at *Brierfield*. Neither of
them was well; they needed a rest and were grateful
to find two of the *Brierfield* carriages awaiting them
when they landed at *Hurricane*. In cordial welcome,
the family at *Hurricane* had prepared the parlor and
tea room for them and had even provided a crib for
the baby. After spending one night in Joseph's home,
they left the next day for *Brierfield*. On May 12, Jef-

ferson wrote his father-in-law with some relief, "I have the pleasure of announcing our arrival at home." [1]

Varina found that absenteeism had its problems. She wrote:

> . . . the destruction I cannot speak of. All of the locks spoilt, sheets cut up for napkins, towels and napkins swept from the land—nothing even to cook in—nothing but fruit trees which was not destroyed. I just sat down, and cried. And so would Jeff I am sure, if he could. However, we concluded not to get anything new we could avoid. The whole family have been forced to sleep without bars [against] the mosquitoes ever since we got here. I have even got to furnish the negroes with summer clothes. . . .
>
> I wish you had a bunch of my flowers—they are splendid, what of them is left. And I shall have so much fruit I cannot use it all this summer—expect it every week. Can you send me up a bundle of fig cuttings in wet moss next week by the boat? [2]

Yet, in this minor desolation, Varina was planning to summer on the Gulf Coast or in the mountain "Knobs of Tennessee." By August, she had indeed gone to Mississippi City near Handsboro where she and Jefferson purchased several favorably situated lots covered with liveoaks, pines, and magnolias. With

[1] Strode, *Jefferson Davis: Private Letters*, p. 87.
[2] *Ibid.*, pp. 89–91.

some hint of pride in their financial circumstances, Varina admitted they had paid a high price for the property—$2,000, of which $1,000 was paid in cash. She also contemplated purchasing another large adjacent lot.[3] The purchase of this property was in no way connected with *Beauvoir*, which they acquired years later.

About this time Varina was occasionally sending money to her mother, and Jefferson had voluntarily offered to educate Varina's younger brother. Jefferson also allowed Joseph the use of $10,000 surplus cash which was being held by his commission merchant. Except for the chronic difficulty of finding and keeping a competent overseer, matters at *Brierfield* were going well.

While Varina vacationed on the Mississippi Coast, Jefferson was busy with the crops and management of *Brierfield*. As a result of close attention, he had been able to "redeem a great part of the crop" for 1857 and had employed another overseer.[4] Although the gnats that year were very worrisome, in October all hands were busy picking cotton. The year's crop proved moderately successful, and the prospect was favorable.

By December 16, 1857, Senator Davis had returned to his work in Washington. The family remained in the capital city through the spring and summer of 1858, and during September vacationed in Maine. In

---

[3] *Ibid.*, p. 93.
[4] *Ibid.*

November, while Varina remained in Washington, Jefferson returned to *Brierfield* to attend to business affairs at the end of the crop year. News from the plantation was not good. Jefferson "found everything in a very unsatisfactory state at home and *scant half a crop*." [5] Because of considerable flooding, 1858 had been a poor crop year.

Beginning in January, 1859, *Brierfield* endured bad weather with constant rain. Although the plowing had been started, progress was slow and the ground was not in good order. The planting schedule was running late. Only the stock was in good shape, and the hands were busy building log cribs and pens. In Washington, Jefferson was very busy in the Senate, working from early morning until late every night. Sectional tensions were increasing.

In Mississippi the Big River rose steadily and ominously until high water threatened *Brierfield*. The urgency required Jefferson's presence at home. He left the capital on March 16, and seven days later arrived at the Bend. He wrote his mother-in-law, Mrs. William B. Howell: "The river here is high and rising rapidly. Our levees have been improved but the excessive rains have injured our prospect for a crop, and greatly embarrass us by destroying the pasturage on which we have been accustomed to rely." [6]

[5] *Ibid.*, p. 100.
[6] *Ibid.*, pp. 103–104.

Prosperity and Adversity

Varina, in Washington, was concerned about *Brierfield* but was reconciled to the fact that the roses in the garden could not be trimmed until fall, when new ones might be planted. If at all possible, she hoped the new asparagus bed could be dressed and replenished and the strawberry plants divided. The quinces, too, needed cultivation.

Jefferson stubbornly fought the flood. Day and night he labored to protect the acres he had claimed from the wilderness. On April 23, he moved his livestock to the high hills of Grand Gulf, several miles downriver on the Mississippi side. He would not think of leaving until he had made provision for the safety of his Negroes. Unwilling to send them away, he considered moving the women and children to a higher and safer place should the danger increase. Shortly, the entire Bend was inundated. Jefferson could get in a boat at the front steps of *Brierfield* and row over the water-covered cotton fields all the way to the back steps of *Hurricane*.[7] His property was a lake.

Distressed about the plantation and concerned about Varina, who in Washington had given birth to another son, Jefferson reported: "The water runs with strong current across the main ridge which was dry in the flood of 1828, and was considered above any possible rise of the river." [8] All of these problems plagued Davis

[7] *Ibid.*, p. 108.
[8] *Ibid.*

while he was drastically economizing and hoping to increase production in order to recoup the losses he had suffered as the result of the poor crop the previous year.

Varina, at this crucial period, was depressed because Jefferson wanted to name their new baby boy for his brother Joseph. She wanted to name the baby for her father. Although she grudgingly admitted Jefferson's right to name the baby, she could never approve of his choice and confided to her mother: "I could never participate in paying in my opinion, the highest compliment in a woman's power to a man whose very name was only suggestive to me of injustice and unkindness from my youth up to middle age. . . . I don't abuse Jeff's brother, but I came so close to hating him that I should hate mightily to be as near to the edge of a precipice, for I am afraid I shall fall off. . . ." [9] Nevertheless, the boy was christened Joseph.

In May the flood receded sufficiently for Jefferson to return to Washington long enough to settle his family at a summer resort near Oakland, Maryland. He hastened back to *Brierfield* in late June to supervise the rehabilitation of the devastated plantation. As he expected, much work was to be done. Some late cotton was raised and the levees were repaired. On November 24, Jefferson was still at *Brierfield*. Shipment of the cotton had been delayed, Jefferson told a friend,

[9] *Ibid.*, p. 110.

because "we have made very little and have ginned none; for this there are two reasons; first, the chute is so low that we have no opportunity to ship from the usual landing, and second, the mules are employed in repairing levees." [10] The year 1859 had been very bad indeed for *Brierfield*. Nevertheless, when Congress convened in December, Jefferson Davis was at his post of duty in the Senate.

Davis' absence, erratic management after the death of James Pemberton, bad weather, and the flood had adversely affected *Brierfield*. The cotton yield in 1857 had been disappointing, only half a crop matured in 1858, and in 1859 there was virtually none—only indescribable destruction. The decline would never be substantially reversed, in spite of temporary improvement during 1860.

Years later, in 1878, the Supreme Court of Mississippi found that "in 1860 there were largely more than a hundred slaves on 'Brierfield,' which with other personal property there, must have been worth $100,000. The annual cotton crop was from 400 to 450 bales, worth more than $20,000 per annum. . . . The residence at 'Brierfield' was expensive, and fitted up with marble mantels—a thing unusual in country homes in this State. The grounds were adorned with shrubs and trees imported from foreign lands." [11] Although

[10] *Ibid.*, p. 112.
[11] Davis v. Bomar, 55 Mississippi Reports, pp. 773–774.

this retrospective generalization correctly portrayed *Brierfield's* best years, it would have more nearly described the plantation as it was in 1856 than in 1860. Had other events not intervened, *Brierfield* would have quickly recovered from the flood of 1859, because it possessed the necessary physical and personal resources. A comeback had definitely been started during 1860, but there were even more disastrous days ahead.

CHAPTER VIII

Unwelcome Notice

THE TERRIFYING imminence of national disruption filled 1860 with feverish activity. Jefferson Davis was caught up in the midst of the brewing storm, and senatorial burdens consumed his total energy. Superimposed on the national scene were the disastrous rupture of the Democratic Party and the emergence of a determined Republican Party. That fall, Davis returned to Warren County to vote for a President in the November 6 election. After Lincoln's victory was announced, Davis attempted to do whatever he could to forestall disintegration of the country.

On December 20, 1860, South Carolina bolted from the Union. The crisis at Charleston rose to a climax, and Mississippi seceded on January 9, 1861. After he received official notice of his state's secession, Jefferson Davis withdrew from the Senate on January 21 and made his moving farewell address. He and Varina stayed in Washington for a week and then undertook the four or five day journey to Jackson, where Jefferson Davis was commissioned General of Mississippi Volunteers, a position he deemed most suited to his abilities. The Davises remained in Jackson for almost a week, while the General attended to many necessary and urgent details of preparing for the war he predicted to be inevitable. They had arrived in Jackson about February 1 and finally reached *Brierfield* either February 6 or 7. They believed the remote plantation, almost surrounded by water, would provide sanctuary for Varina and their children while Jefferson was away on his military duties. Surely, thought Varina, war if it came would never touch secluded *Brierfield*.

Spring had come early. Yellow jonquils, violets, and camellias bloomed profusely, and tender green leaf buds laced the trees. The air stirred gentle and fragrant; the earth grew warm and ready to conceive. But *Brierfield* did not look neat and well kept as it had formerly. "There was no James Pemberton to trim its hedges and repair its fences. The Cherokee rose with which the roadways were bordered . . . had been allowed to trail." [1] The house, buildings, and gardens had suffered from the flood and, to some degree, from neglect. The first order of business, however, was not to renovate the house but to repair and restore the levees and make the field productive again.

Some of the neglect was Varina's. She had learned

[1] Eron Rowland, *Varina Howell, Wife of Jefferson Davis* (New York: The Macmillan Company, 1927), p. 437.

to enjoy her Washington friends and capital society, and her high position as a Cabinet wife had given her a prominence and preference that drew her inside the exciting inner circle of national affairs. At *Brierfield*, she was isolated. She did not enjoy the company of Joseph Davis or members of his household. For eight years, Varina had seldom returned to *Brierfield* with Jefferson. The children had demanded much of her time, and traveling with them was difficult. She preferred to spend the recesses between Congressional sessions at the seaside or other resort places in the East. Jefferson Davis had returned each fall to attend to the crops and the plantation business; but *Brierfield* had become a man's world, without the woman's touches that insure maintenance of the warmth and comfort essential to a home.

Now, however, the Davises had been abruptly cut off from the world beyond the South—the old associations and friends on the Potomac. *Brierfield* was once more home. Varina would live there while Jefferson was away.

Much work had to be accomplished during this time of tension and urgency. The plantation Negroes readily accepted from Davis the charge to protect Varina and the children and to defend the home while he was gone. The task of making the place more habitable loomed large. Reclamation of the lawns and gardens was undertaken and the fences and buildings were repaired. No longer were there long days of rest and relaxation and a placid rural world free from care. Varina worked with her husband closely, giving her full attention to farming affairs so that she could carry on after he left.

The Davises had been home scarcely three or four days when the most dramatic event ever to happen at *Brierfield* occurred on February 10, 1861. Jefferson Davis was notified that he had been elected President of the Confederacy. He and Varina were alone in the garden when they received the message.

Jefferson Davis later recorded the unadorned facts. On one occasion he commented: "I went to my home in Warren County in order to prepare for what I believed was to be a long and severe struggle. Soon a messenger came from the Provisional Confederate Congress at Montgomery, bringing the unwelcome notice that I had been elected Provisional President of the Confederate States." [2] He wrote another very similar version of receiving the message: "I had gone to my home, Brierfield in Warren County, and had begun, in the homely but expressive language of Mr. Clay, 'to repair my fences.' While thus engaged, notice was received of my election to the Presidency of the Confederate States, with an urgent request to pro-

[2] J. William Jones, *The Davis Memorial Volume* (Richmond, Va.: B. F. Johnson and Co., Publishers, 1890), p. 38.

ceed immediately to Montgomery for inauguration." [3]

In her *Memoir*, Mrs. Davis has recorded her impressions at the time: "The messenger with the notification that Mr. Davis had been elected President . . . found him in our garden assisting to make rose-cuttings; when reading the telegram he looked so grieved that I feared some evil had befallen our family. After a few minutes' painful silence he told me, as a man might speak of a sentence of death. As he neither desired nor expected the position, he was more deeply depressed than before." [4]

Drawing on "conversations with contemporaries" —including, perhaps, Mrs. Davis in her later years— Mrs. Eron Rowland in *Varina Howell, Wife of Jefferson Davis* elaborated somewhat more romantically:

> On this special morning they [Jefferson and Varina] were pruning a prized rose bush—a magnificent tea, bearing the name of "The Glory of France" several of which grew on the grounds, one she says, by the side of the gate. The parent bush had been brought from the garden at "The Briers" near Natchez, after they had returned from their honeymoon. This special variety had survived neglect and her husband had decided to graft some of the healthiest slips upon other stocks. They were, she wrote, ex-

[3] Jefferson Davis, *Rise and Fall of the Confederate Government* (New York: D. Appleton and Company, 1881), I, 230; and Varina Howell Davis, *Jefferson Davis, Ex-President*, II, 18.
[4] Varina Howell Davis, *Jefferson Davis, Ex-President*, II, 18–19.

amining a handful of vigorous branches, cutting away the shoots to a tender bud to be used for the graft when a messenger on horseback arrived with a telegram.[5]

There is some doubt, however, whether the messenger arrived in the morning, as Mrs. Rowland has indicated. Hudson Strode is undoubtedly correct when he places the event in the afternoon.[6] From Vicksburg to *Brierfield*, eighteen miles over a dusty dirt road, was ordinarily a full day's horseback ride. The dispatch from Montgomery apparently reached the telegraph office in Vicksburg soon after it was opened on the morning of February 10. The manager promptly employed a "messenger with horse" and instructed him to "speed the distance, deliver the document, await reply and return without loss of time." [7] Even assuming the rider sped the distance in half the usual time, probably changing horses about halfway at or near Warrenton, it would have been early afternoon before he could have possibly delivered the message at *Brierfield*. Particularly significant is the fact that the hurrying horseman did not return to the office in Vicksburg until "a little after midnight." [8] These facts strongly suggest that the message must

---

[5] Rowland, *Varina Howell, Wife*, pp. 441–442.
[6] Strode, *Jefferson Davis: American Patriot*, p. 401.
[7] *Ibid.*, footnote 2.
[8] *Ibid.*

have been delivered to Jefferson Davis during the early part of the afternoon.

Duty prevailed over personal wish, and Jefferson Davis did not waiver or hesitate. He decided promptly to accept the unwanted task, and from his rose garden dispatched his reply by the same messenger who had delivered the summons. There was very little time to attend to the multitudinous details of necessary business before his departure. The plantation bell was rung to summon all the hands, and, as Varina recalled, "he assembled his negroes and made them an affectionate farewell speech, to which they responded with expressions of devotion, and he left home next day for Mongomery." [9]

Varina started packing his things immediately. As the twilight shadows deepened on *Brierfield* "a few hours later," Varina stood reflecting on the wide front gallery while Jefferson Davis "sat silent in deep thought in his library." [10] After a short and restless night, the morning of February 11, 1861, dawned. All the family members and servants gathered again to bid the master farewell.

After embracing the members of his family, Jefferson Davis crossed the front porch and descended the steps, exchanging handshakes and words of confidence and affection with those gathered there. He mounted

[9] Varina Howell Davis, *Jefferson Davis, Ex-President*, II, 19.
[10] Rowland, *Varina Howell, Wife*, p. 443.

his horse, took a long look at his home, and rode toward the landing through the tall shading trees and over the wide fields he had cleared. There was no turning back.

Isaiah T. Montgomery, a young Negro who would years later with his father and brother purchase *Brierfield*, found the town of Mound Bayou, and become a member of the Mississippi Constitutional Convention of 1890, rode with him to the river. Captain Tom Leathers' great steamboat *Natchez* was due up river any minute. Since the landings at *Brierfield* and *Hurricane* could not accommodate the *Natchez*, Jefferson and Isaiah rode to a landing three miles downriver from *Brierfield*. When they reached the Big River, they rowed out to meet the *Natchez*. Hearing the steamer blow for the lower landing, they knew they could not make it in time. Jefferson directed the rowboat to a mid-river island, and as the puffing steamboat churned upstream, he stood up in his little boat and hailed Captain Leathers to take him aboard the *Natchez*.

The steamboat responded with a mighty, deep-chested blast that reverberated throughout the surrounding forests and across the swirling waters. The occupants of *Brierfield* heard the blast and knew that Jefferson Davis was on his way to become President of the Confederacy. They listened to the diminishing sound of the *Natchez* as it saluted the *Brierfield* and

Hurricane landings, New Carthage and Palmyra, until the vessel glided beyond hearing toward Vicksburg. From the steamboat, Jefferson Davis must have turned toward the shore for one more look at the *Brierfield* frontage. Certainly he glimpsed the high gables atop the majestic house at *Hurricane*. This view would be his last of the great mansion, for in little more than a year it would be ashes.

Varina, who planned to follow Jefferson to Montgomery within ten days, plunged into the gigantic task of preparing the plantation and its people for another departure of its owners from home—a departure much more significant than previous ones. Jefferson's valuable and extensive library was carefully packed and later sent "inland" to another Davis plantation house between Bolton and Raymond, Mississippi. In spite of these precautions, the books would ultimately be completely destroyed.

On February 18, 1861, at Montgomery, Alabama, Jefferson Davis was inaugurated as President of the Confederacy. Mrs. Rowland has recalled that, when Jefferson's address reached Davis Bend, Varina read the inaugural message to her father and Joseph E. Davis, who were spending a few days with her at *Brierfield*. Mrs. Rowland wrote: "Together they sat in the pleasant library and listened spell bound as she read. At a number of paragraphs the two men stood up, cheered and clapped their hands frantically. As she continued to read slowly each passage with her heart beating so fiercely she could feel it throbbing against her breast, her eyes were at times blinded with tears. When it was finished the old men stood up again and cheered so wildly that it brought from the fields a number of the negroes and white laborers panting with fear that the house was on fire." [11] No more cheers would ring through *Brierfield's* halls. After that night, the Old South died at *Brierfield.*

Varina probably left Davis Bend early in the morning of February 20. She visited her parents in New Orleans briefly and arrived at Montgomery via boat up the Alabama River from Mobile on February 28. *Brierfield* would never again be the Davises' home.

[11] *Ibid.,* p. 454.

CHAPTER IX

War, Recovery, and Sale

THE ACCELERATED work on *Brierfield* which had begun in 1861 was not to be continued. Jefferson could not spare time for plantation affairs; and although Varina had returned in April, 1861, to check matters, her visit was brief. In the spring of 1862, a flood three feet higher than the record crest reached in 1859 covered the *Brierfield* and *Hurricane* lands. The water, which reached an unprecedented height, probably even invaded the house at *Brierfield*.

When control of the Mississippi River became a prime military objective of the Union military and naval forces, *Brierfield* was no longer a remote and secluded Shangri-la immune from exposure to the war. Admiral Farragut, with a strong and determined fleet, pushed north, upriver from New Orleans, opening the waterway to Federal use as he proceeded. When the Union forces reached Grand Gulf and Davis Bend, a raiding party burned *Hurricane* on June 24, 1862. Although the raiders also prowled through *Brierfield*, for some strange reason they refrained from applying the torch to the house. As a productive unit, however, *Brierfield* had become thoroughly disorganized because of flood and war. When he was unable to capture strongly fortified Vicksburg, Farragut retreated downriver to New Orleans, leaving the river in Confederate hands from Vicksburg to Port Hudson.

Finally realizing that the Mississippi River and its environs would be a major thoroughfare strongly coveted and staunchly defended, Joseph Davis, with Jefferson's approval, at the outset of the war bought two hill farms farther inland in the vicinity of Bolton, Edwards, and Raymond, Mississippi. Anticipating further trouble at Davis Bend, Joseph moved his family and as many of the *Hurricane* and *Brierfield* slaves as he could to *Fleetwood*, as the new place was named. Just before the raid on *Brierfield*, Jefferson Davis' parlor furniture, his books, and family correspondence had also been taken there for safekeeping. At best, this move was a makeshift arrangement. The new farm was far less comfortable and the land far less productive than that on the river. With a handful of help, Ben Montgomery, an intelligent slave of Joseph Davis, stayed on the Bend as overseer and tried his best to protect and hold the plantation together. In January, 1863, Ben reported that 300 bushels of corn had been harvested. His main concern was to produce as much food and firewood as possible.

Grant initiated his thrust for Vicksburg from Memphis early in 1863. Farragut cooperated in this maneuver by renewing his surge upriver from the south. In May, 1863, *Brierfield* was revisted by Federal troops. James W. Garner has written that "when Farragut's fleet steamed up the river in 1863, it stopped long enough to allow the marines to go ashore and destroy or carry away everything of value." [1]

On June 1, 1863, a Vicksburg newspaper reported that Yankees had rifled *Brierfield*, destroyed all farming implements, as well as household and kitchen furniture, and badly defaced the premises. Pictures were probably then taken of "the House Jeff Built." These events occurred during the prolonged siege when most Confederate soldiers in the area were bottled up in Vicksburg.

After the fall of Vicksburg on July 4, 1863, the Union Army took control of *Brierfield* and *Hurricane*. According to a letter from Elmer D. Parker, "War Department records in the National Archives show that Brierfield Plantation, Warren County, Mississippi . . . owned by Jefferson Davis . . . consisted of 1,000 acres, one mansion and ten quarters. It was re-

[1] James Wilford Garner, *Reconstruction in Mississippi* (Gloucester, Mass.: Peter Smith, 1964), p. 252.

served for the use of the Bureau of Refugees, Freedmen and Abandoned Lands," [2] known as the "Freedmen's Bureau."

Martha Mitchell Bigelow has commented that "one of the most interesting experiments was the one on Jefferson Davis' plantation at Davis Bend. Here some seventy lessees, all Negroes, seemed to have been more successful than the Northern speculators. The good showing of the Negroes at Davis Bend was due in part to the excellent training given by Joe and Jefferson Davis to their slaves before the war. This colony led by the Montgomerys eventually became the all Negro colony of Mound Bayou." [3] Professor Bigelow also pointed out that in 1864 the "Jeff Davis Mansion" was headquarters for the Cincinnati Contraband Relief Commission of the Freedmen's Aid Society. On the entire 10,000 acre Davis Bend Colony, the Home Farm in Mississippi, there were 1,750 freedmen at one time; and the project cleared $160,000 in 1865. The *Brierfield* part of the colony produced 234 bales of cotton for a profit of $25,000. [4]

The havoc and destruction of war were finally ter-

[2] Elmer O. Parker for Robert W. Krauskopf, Chief Army and Navy Branch, General Services Administration, National Archives and Records Service, Washington, D. C., letter to the author, March 23, 1966.

[3] Martha Mitchell Bigelow, "Vicksburg: Experiment in Freedom," *Journal of Mississippi History*, XXVI (February, 1964), 42–43.

[4] Garner, *Reconstruction in Missisippi*, p. 258.

minated in April, 1865; and Jefferson Davis, still resisting, was captured in Georgia and harshly imprisoned at Fortress Monroe, Virginia. His own future and that of his property were most uncertain. Realizing his brother's precarious situation, the elderly Joseph E. Davis initiated action to recover his property from the government. In a typically positive and forthright manner, Joseph, on September 22, 1865, applied directly to Andrew Johnson, President of the United States, disdaining to go through channels. He stated his case briefly but with a hint of impatience:

> I am advised that, to have my home and property restored, it will be necessary for me to apply to the president of the United States, and to get some person of influence at Washington to present my claim. I have no friends in Washington to whom I could apply, nor the means of making such. I must, therefore, rely upon the justice of my claim. In the year 1818 I purchased of the United States some lands on the Mississippi River, below the Walnut Hills, now Vicksburg; upon the land I fixed my residence and occupied it forty years.[5]

Joseph Davis had never given Jefferson a formal deed to Brierfield. As his brother-in-law, William Stamps, commented, "He had the peculiarity of rarely, or never, giving deeds when he gave or sold land to his relations." [6] Joseph was also determined that if

[5] Davis v. Bomar, 55 Mississippi Reports, p. 716.
[6] *Ibid.*, p. 699.

anything happened to Jefferson, neither Varina nor her parents, the Howells, would ever hold title to the property. As events developed, the circumstance of record title in Joseph's name could be used to salvage *Brierfield* as well as *Hurricane*.

Jefferson, sensing that such an advantage might exist and doubting that any property held in his name would ever be restored, made the following cautious and pertinent suggestion to Joseph in a letter written to Varina on October 20, 1865: "Brother Joe should not, I think, return to the river place. All is changed. He will be troubled beyond his strength by the confusion that must exist. An agent will suit the new regime much better than the old one. If he goes back, why not take the Brierfield house? He can claim possession as owner of the land. But my decided opinion is, in the existing condition, neither he nor Lize should stay there." [7]

As if to fortify his legal claim to *Brierfield* should he die before consummating the recovery, Joseph wrote a will on September 26, 1865, devising to the children of Jefferson Davis the *Brierfield Plantation* and declaring that *Brierfield* was actually a part of *Hurricane Plantation*. Joseph probably thought this action would satisfy the government and at the same time by-pass Varina and the Howells. Several years later, Joseph prepared and executed another will replacing this one.

[7] *Ibid.*, p. 717.

Although almost impoverished, the older brother was still spirited and unsubdued. When he thought certain high army officers of the Freedmen's Bureau were unduly demanding "levies" against him before releasing *Hurricane*, the outraged old man made charges of blackmail and fraud against the officers and demanded that they be court martialed. Otherwise, Joseph might have recovered his property sooner.

As soon as she was free to leave Georgia, where she had been detained after Jefferson was taken into custody, Varina in March, 1866, hastened to Vicksburg to see about *Brierfield* and its people. Coming up from New Orleans, the steamboat on which she had passage touched briefly at the *Brierfield* and *Hurricane* landings; but Varina did not disembark, and she could not see much of the places from the boat. In Vicksburg, she visited the aging Joseph Davis. Mutual trouble had brought them closer together. After learning that *Brierfield* was in the custody of Federal authorities, Varina decided not to go to the plantation, and she despaired of recovering any of their possessions. She soon left Vicksburg for a reunion with Jefferson at the prison in Virginia.

On September 8, 1866, Joseph E. Davis persistently renewed his demand for possession of his land to General Wood, Commander of the Military Department of Mississippi and Assistant Commissioner of the Freedmen's Bureau, stating: "I would respectfully ask to be placed in possession of my plantation, known as 'Hurricane' and 'Brierfield,' situated in Warren County, Miss." [8] In accordance with Jefferson's suggestion, Joseph specifically included *Brierfield* in this request. To his application Joseph attached certificates showing title held in his name. Jefferson was still in prison.

A year had elapsed since his first letter to President Johnson, and Joseph felt it was time for more effective action, particularly since his pardon had been granted. He turned to his friend, Dr. J. H. D. Bomar, who before the war had given up his medical practice to engage in farming. The fortune he had amassed was lost when the Confederacy fell, and since that time he had turned to real estate development. Dr. Bomar was wise, intelligent, and discreet; he could be fully trusted.

The details of how *Brierfield* and *Hurricane* were recovered were first related by Dr. Bomar as testimony in court:

> I was called on by Joseph E. Davis to present to General Wood his application for the restoration of Hurricane and Brierfield plantations, and was afterwards employed to go to Washington to see President Johnson about the restoration of the property. When Joseph E. Davis first made application to General Wood, I asked him about "Brierfield." He simply answered, "The title is in me." [9]

[8] *Ibid.*, p. 716.
[9] *Ibid.*, p. 708.

War, Recovery, and Sale

When Bomar told Joseph it would be necessary to show title, Joseph replied that the title was in him, that he had never conveyed it. Dr. Bomar's testimony continued as follows:

> I supposed that all he wanted was to get possession of the land. My impression was that he wanted to protect his brother from loss by confiscation. There was reason to conceal from the Federals any right that Jefferson Davis had to the land. Mr. Davis was in prison, and it was generally believed that his property would be confiscated, if nothing worse happened. Joseph E. Davis claimed and received "Brierfield" as his own. He claimed and received rents from the date of his pardon, 28th March, 1866. General Howard first sent his adjutant to let me know that he was not satisfied with the evidence of title as to "Brierfield." He thought that Jefferson Davis owned that place. I told the adjutant that I had certificates from the clerk of the court that there was no record of any conveyance from Joseph E. Davis of any property, and that, if required, I would go to the land-office and show him that patents had issued to Joseph E. Davis for lands including those of "Brierfield." Joseph E. Davis said nothing about his brother's property being confiscated, or about protecting him from loss by confiscation; it was my own impression that Joseph E. Davis wanted to protect his brother—not from anything that he said, except his answering, "The title is in me." [10]

[10] *Ibid.*, pp. 708–709.

At the end of the war, *Hurricane* and *Brierfield* were in possession of the United States as abandoned lands. Many persons expected that the properties would be confiscated; but President Andrew Johnson, who was said to be personally friendly to Joseph E. Davis, sent him a pardon in September, 1866. Although the pardon was dated March, 1866, it was detained and not delivered until six months after its issuance.

Interviewing General Howard about the lands, Dr. Bomar found him piqued and hostile because Joseph had charged him with fraud, mismanagement, and mistreatment of the Negroes remaining on Davis Bend. Bomar proved to be an adroit emissary when he appealed to General Howard on the basis that the actual merits of the cause should prevail over anger and personal ill will. The men finally agreed that Joseph should receive rent for the land from the time of his pardon. Dr. Bomar successfully carried his point that the date of the pardon controlled over the delayed time of delivery. Winning this point added $15,000 to Joseph Davis' account.

Although Joseph was refused immediate possession, General Howard did agree to re-entry on January 1, 1867, only three months after his interview with Dr. Bomar. When Dr. Bomar appealed to the President on behalf of Joseph for earlier possession, Andrew Johnson declined to intervene because he was laboring under great embarrassment from his enemies, who were seeking any pretext to injure him. The decision for possession on January 1, 1867, was, therefore, accepted, and Joseph E. Davis was delighted with the settlement. Dr. Bomar requested permission to visit Jefferson Davis at his prison in Fortress Monroe, but when his request was denied, Dr. Bomar returned to Vicksburg.[11]

The question has been raised whether the repossession of *Brierfield* on the assertion of title in Joseph Davis was honorable and proper or fraudulent. The Supreme Court of Mississippi in 1878 answered this problem positively. Judge H. H. Chalmers stated: "Joseph . . . simply took advantage of the outstanding record title in himself to recover the land for his brother . . ." He continued: "Fictitious claims and conveyances of property among the adherents of unsuccessful rebellions, in order to save it from confiscation, have marked the history of all ages and countries. We are not aware that the sternest historians or the most austere moralists have ever regarded them as indicative of personal dishonor." [12]

After obtaining the government commitment, Joseph Davis wasted no time. Since he was unable to operate the land himself and apprehensive of some

[11] J. H. D. Bomar, autobiographical memorandum, supplied by his grandson, the late J. B. Dabney.
[12] Davis v. Bomar, 55 Mississippi Reports, pp. 775–776.

further attempt at confiscation, Joseph looked for a purchaser. An unexpected prospective buyer appeared —Ben Montgomery, a former Davis slave. Intelligent and quick to learn, Ben had proved to be adept in business and proficient in almost anything he tried. When he had worked as a slave on Joseph Davis' plantation, his master had trained and encouraged him and given him a great deal of business latitude and responsibility. Recalling that she had known Ben Montgomery when she visited *Hurricane* after her marriage (probably in 1844), Mrs. Roach has written a brief account of him:

> My first knowledge of him was as a merchant and his Master's agent to ship cotton, and transact all his Master's business with the steamboats of the period. Ben's store, and dwelling house, were near the steamboat landing and warehouse. His wife lived "at home," sewed occasionally for the ladies of the family, but usually only kept house for her husband. Ben brought goods from N. O. and Natchez in his own name; his Master having once guaranteed him, he preserved his own credit. The ladies of the family used to "shop" at his store, which was well supplied with necessary dry goods of the time, as well as staple goods. Mr. Davis visited us once when he brought Ben, ostensibly as his valet, but really to get your father to permit him to go through the Machine Shops to see all there was to be seen there. Ben waited on his Master, and asked permission of me to wait on the table, which he did most dexterously. . . . In 1853

Ben sent quantities of foods, meal, eggs, and every thing that could be sent to us for the yellow fever patients, and wrote your father such beautiful letters with the supplies sent for our sick. In '54 and '55 he also sent supplies. His Master was not at home on these occasions.[13]

When Jefferson Davis became President of the Confederacy and Joseph had to move away from the river for safety, Ben was left in charge of *Brierfield* and *Hurricane* plantations. After Davis Bend was seized by the Union Army, Ben Montgomery was entrusted with the major responsibility of controlling the large Negro colony established there by the Freedmen's Bureau.

Ben had two sons, Isaiah and Thornton. Joseph and Jefferson recognized their abilities and afforded them maximum educational opportunities. Isaiah, in particular, proved efficient at clerical and office work. Once they had been emancipated, Ben and his sons were ambitious to improve themselves and become landowners. Realizing that Joseph had recovered *Brierfield* and *Hurricane* and might be interested in selling the properties, the Montgomerys made a proposal of purchase to Joseph E. Davis. Dr. Bomar's successful trip to Washington in September, with a commitment to possession on January 1, had opened the way for immediate negotiations for sale of the land. There was

[13] Roach memorandum, August 22, 1897.

still no assurance, however, that further steps toward nullifying the President's action would not be taken by a vengeful Congress. The Davises might yet lose their land.

Joseph worked out a deal. Benjamin L. Montgomery, backed by his sons Isaiah and Thornton, would pay $300,000 for "4,000 acres," the asserted total of *Brierfield* and *Hurricane*. The principal would be payable over a period of nine years, with the last payment being due on January 1, 1876. Interest at 6 percent per annum, amounting to $18,000.00, would be paid on January 1 of each year, beginning in January, 1867. There was to be no down payment.[14]

Seventy-five dollars per acre was a good price for the land, and the annual interest payments would provide a fair income. Neither Jefferson, because he was in prison, nor Joseph, because of his advanced age, could look after the plantations. The Montgomerys' former masters offered them a good opportunity; and if they paid the stipulated price, Joseph and Jefferson would fare well financially. At the same time, Joseph believed it would be good protection against possible confiscation to have the land in control of the Negroes who were favored by the national government.

If the purchasers failed to pay, the Davis brothers or their heirs would likely recover the land after the

[14] Warren County, Miss., Land Records, Office of Chancery Clerk. Deed Book VV, p. 14.

passions of war cooled. At least, they could reasonably expect to receive the interest payments each year, even if the principal were not reduced. Josph E. Davis executed a deed to Ben Montgomery for both pieces of land on November 19, 1866, and took a mortgage to protect the payments. Some years later, the Supreme Court found that "either at the time of the sale, or sometime afterwards (Montgomery made two statements as to the time), Joseph E. Davis stipulated with the vendees that if Jefferson should ever be released, and should desire to reoccupy 'Brierfield,' the sale as to it should be rescinded." [15]

Joseph promptly sought Jefferson's approval of the sale through Mrs. Mary Stamps, widow of a nephew of the two brothers, who was soon to visit Jefferson in prison. Joseph met her in Jackson and charged her "to tell Jefferson that, as the duration of his then imprisonment was uncertain, he had acted for him, in the sale of 'Brierfield' for what he considered his best interest; that the sale was made subject to his [Jefferson's] approval; and he expressed an earnest desire that his brother should communicate with him on the subject." [16]

Mary Stamps hand delivered to Joseph the following memorandum from Jefferson Davis dated December 17, 1866:

[15] Davis v. Bomar, 55 Mississippi Reports, p. 777.
[16] *Ibid.*, p. 777.

In default of being permitted to correspond, I requested Varina to inform you that any arrangements which you made with Ben would, of course, be agreeable to me. This I supposed you would anticipate; but as you had expressed a wish to that effect, the announcement was made as above. It will, no doubt, occur to you that, the proceeding having been made public, it will be advisable to close it soon, and tightly, lest the desire for plunder and the active malignity towards you, as my brother, should prompt to some congressional movement to interfere with it. Unless the negroes exceed my expectations, they will never complete the payments. Then it may be that a better state of affairs will render the property valuable to your heirs.[17]

So the sale of the Davis Bend plantations was concluded. It was bona fide in every respect. If the agreement worked out, the Davis brothers would be well compensated. If the Montgomerys defaulted later, they would probably have had the land long enough for the threat of confiscation to have been removed or at least reduced, and the Davises would ultimately stand a chance to repossess their land. Fortunately for the Davises, Ben Montgomery took possession of *Brierfield* and *Hurricane* on January 1, 1867, because radical passions were rising in Congress. The Reconstruction Acts were passed on March 2.

As if to punctuate the end of one era and the be-

[17] *Ibid.*, p. 718.

ginning of another, the great river heaved and changed. The winter of 1866–67 was characterized by rain and snow of unusual intensity in the Ohio Valley. The first rise on the Mississippi River began in February, and by the later part of the month the river was at full stage. In March, a widespread series of furious rainstorms occurred throughout virtually the entire Mississippi watershed, particularly in the headwaters of the Ohio and Tennessee rivers. Rises almost unprecedented in rapidity and height followed. The crest of the first rise reached a stage one foot above the high water of 1859, and a later rise exceeded this record by several inches.

In 1859, when the flood ran across the Davis peninsula, the neck was narrowed and the swale began to widen. During the war, in 1862, the water had poured over the weakened levees three feet higher than it had in 1859. The stronger wash upon the land became more pronounced before the river subsided. Finally in 1867, the saturated, soft soil could no longer retain the urgent, sudden surging of the river, and the irresistible current burst through the crumbling banks. The mighty Mississippi changed course, cutting athwart the end of the giant loop, an avulsion of awesome magnitude. Davis Bend became Davis Island. The old days were gone.

On May 14, 1867, Jefferson Davis was released from Fort Monroe to prepare for his trial in Richmond, Virginia. Because the trial was delayed, he was free to move about for the first time since his capture. Strongly confirming the understanding that the sale of *Brierfield* by Joseph was contingent on Jefferson's not desiring to reclaim his place, Ben Montgomery wrote Joseph Davis on December 5, 1867:

> If you think it at all probable that Mass Jeff will return to "Brierfield" the ensuing year, I should be glad to know, so as to avoid any conflict of arrangements. Billy Mick is the only one of the "Brierfield" people that will make anything; and whatever arrangement is made with parties working on either place, I wish to be able to guarantee their undisturbed possession for the year.
>
> Your ob't serv't,
Ben.[18]

After Christmas, in the early part of 1868, Jefferson and Varina were welcomed in New Orleans. They came upriver through the new cut-off to Vicksburg. Hudson Strode has described their first visit to *Brierfield* since their departure for Montgomery in February, 1861.

> At Vicksburg Davis saw with his own eyes the destruction wrought by the Union army. But he rejoiced that his aged brother, despite his crushing reverses in fortune, was in good spirits. Joseph Davis

[18] *Ibid.*, p. 723.

seemed relieved that he no longer need feel respon-
sible for the health and happiness of the plantation
Negroes. Ben Montgomery and his sons now had the
worry and the challenge. Jefferson Davis took a sad
journey to Davis Bend and beheld the damage the
enemy had made there, including the complete destruction of Hurricane. He stayed only a few hours,
greeting the friendly Negroes, who had once been
his "people." Again he felt like a "returning ghost"
as he had when he re-entered Richmond from Fort
Monroe in May, 1867.[19]

Although Jefferson had expected the interest on the
sale of his property to provide him with an income,
he forgave the Montgomerys the interest for the first
year since they had encountered hard luck because of
floods and both army and boll worms. Rather than
receiving any return from the cotton crop, Davis withdrew funds from his own slim savings to care for the
old Negroes who no longer belonged to him. Hudson
Strode has commented that the "ironies of his return
became as palpable as painful. The place which he
had spent the best years of his life developing into a
model plantation was now possessed by former slaves.
And Negroes were living in his brother's Greek temple library, where he had studied constitutional law
and read world literature. Though the bluecoats had
burned all the books, they had left the building itself

[19] Hudson Strode, *Jefferson Davis: Tragic Hero* (New York: Harcourt, Brace & World, 1964), pp. 326–327.

intact. While Davis had only the most kindly feeling for the Negroes themselves, who for the most part still addressed him as 'Marse Jeff,' he returned to Vicksburg darkly depressed."[20]

Ben Montgomery found it impossible to pay the interest on his purchase. Sometime during 1868, the Montgomerys offered to give up, rescind the purchase, return the property to the Davises, and thus be relieved of their obligation to pay. There is little doubt that Jefferson Davis considered the purchase agreement valid and binding in all respects and in no sense a sham or subterfuge. He was incensed at Ben's proposal and hotly wrote Joseph on December 26, 1868:

> The proposition of Ben and his sons to abandon their contract was preposterous, after having had all its benefits, without having met its obligations. At the time you let them have the land I suppose other purchasers would have been easily found who had capital, at least sufficient to have insured a forfeit to enable them to fulfill their contract. It is no doubt true that the property is too large for the administrative capacity of a negro. It is also within his ability to see that he had better retire with the means he has acquired by the possession of your property, and engage in small trade. It was this course which I expected him in due time to adopt, but supposed it would be done secretly, by covert agents, rather than by direct proposition.[21]

[20] *Ibid.*, p. 327.
[21] Davis v. Bomar, 55 Mississippi Reports, p. 718.

War, Recovery, and Sale

The talented and ambitious Ben Montgomery and his sons had eagerly assumed the calculated risk of owning *Hurricane* and *Brierfield*. From slavery they had reached for instant personal and economic independence, but the responsibilities and hazards had proved to be too formidable.

CHAPTER X

Ordered, Adjudged, and Decreed

BACKED BY JOSEPH'S considerable financial reserves accumulated from a lucrative law practice, the Davis brothers had originally begun *Hurricane* and *Brier-field* on a modest scale and gradually and progressively extended the scope of their operations, always keeping within their resources and reasonable expectations. They built up a certain momentum and reserve as the result of cautious planning and diligent attention. Their success was earned by hard work over a period of years.

Without a reservoir of experience or a financial cushion, Ben Montgomery and his sons seized a timely opportunity and bravely plunged into a full grown project—vast and demanding—during a time of political, economic, and social change producing chaos. Problems created by the river magnified the Montgomerys' burdens and did much to thwart their hopes for success. Just after Ben Montgomery assumed control in 1867, the river changed course, making the

Bend an isolated island. Heavy and damaging floods occurred in 1868, 1871, and 1874. Not surprisingly, therefore, Ben frequently missed the annual interest payments, to the disappointment and financial embarrassment of both Joseph and Jefferson, who had counted on receiving at least the interest each year.

Apparently feeling that the sale to the Montgomerys had circumvented the threat of confiscation, Joseph E. Davis made a new will dated March 3, 1869, revoking his 1865 will specifically devising *Brierfield* as if it were his own property to give. Joseph directed that his executors should extend liberal indulgence to the Montgomerys in their efforts to pay for the property. He also made provision for his two living daughters, Florida and Caroline.

From the $300,000 sale to Ben Montgomery of *Brierfield* and *Hurricane*, Joseph left $150,000 to his grandchildren, Mary Elizabeth and Joseph D. Mitchell, daughter and son of his deceased child Mary; and $20,000 each to the four children of Jefferson Davis. These bequests totaled $230,000, leaving $70,000 from the Montgomery sale unmentioned and without specific disposition. All else and the remainder was devised to Joseph D. Mitchell and Mary Elizabeth, who had married William D. Hamer.[1]

Later, Jefferson would contend that Joseph's silence

[1] Joseph E. Davis Will, Davis v. Bomar, 55 Mississippi Reports, p. 711.

regarding the $70,000 balance indicated that he considered this sum to be the value of *Brierfield*; and, therefore, he had made no attempt to dispose of funds not his to bestow.[2] Others would disagree and assert that the $80,000 designated for Jefferson's children represented the equivalent worth of *Brierfield*.[3]

Under severe financial and physical strain, Jefferson Davis attempted to recover his broken health and find some means of supporting his family. In November, 1869, he accepted a position as president of the Carolina Life Insurance Company and moved to Memphis, Tennessee. Less than a year later, at the advanced age of eighty-six, his brother Joseph, frail but nevertheless strong of heart and mind, died at Vicksburg, September 18, 1870. Along with Dr. J. H. D. Bomar and a Davis nephew, J. D. Smith, Jefferson Davis was named as an executor of Joseph Davis' will. The three men undertook administration of the estate. When Dr. Bomar showed him the will, Jefferson expressed dissatisfaction and intimated "that he did not like for another to be generous with his property or at his expense." [4]

When the severe financial panic of 1873 wrecked the Carolina Life Insurance Company, the financial misfortunes of Jefferson Davis reached disastrous pro-

[2] Davis v. Bomar, 55 Mississippi Reports, p. 725.
[3] *Ibid.*, p. 684.
[4] *Ibid.*, pp. 709, 779.

portions. It became apparent that Ben Montgomery could not pay for *Hurricane* and *Brierfield*. Jefferson would somehow have to reclaim his property or lose it forever. To salvage something from his old property was his last hope.

Yet serious and embarrassing difficulties had developed. Joseph had never made a deed conveying *Brierfield* to Jefferson, and the younger man had never pressed the point with his respected older brother. In fact, they had both taken advantage of this state of the record title to regain the land from the federal government. Most distressing, however, was the fact that Joseph's grandchildren, Mary Elizabeth Mitchell Hamer, affectionately known as Lize, and Joseph Davis Mitchell, without knowledge of the events of earlier years, had come to feel that Joseph's assertions of title were quite genuine. They considered the property or the proceeds therefrom to be rightfully theirs. To reacquire *Brierfield*, Jefferson would be forced to contend with these heirs for whom he held considerable affection.

Furthermore, as an executor of Joseph's will, Jefferson had accepted a trust to support it, and he had acted in such a capacity for more than three years without formal objection. To claim his property now would involve opposition to the estate as well as the heirs of Joseph Davis. Convinced that in all truth and justice *Brierfield* was his alone, Jefferson Davis concluded that he would be disloyal to his own family if he did not assert his ownership and right to the land he had wrested from the wilderness, developed, and now so desperately needed.

Aggravating his monetary crisis was the fact that the other executors of Joseph's will had declined to distribute to Jefferson any funds received from Ben Montgomery and his sons until Jefferson's rights to *Brierfield* had been established in court. Reluctantly, but without any other reasonable alternative, Jefferson decided he could no longer remain silent about *Brierfield*. In view of other circumstances, this was not an auspicious time for Jefferson Davis to seek any relief in the courts. The radical reconstructionists were in power both locally and statewide. The old order which Jefferson symbolized was officially despised. Nevertheless, he had refused to apply for pardon because he believed he had done no wrong.

Davis chose William B. Pittman, who had earned a favorable reputation as "one of the ablest lawyers in the South," for his legal representative. Born in Kentucky, Pittman had attended St. Paul College in Minnesota and had been admitted to the Minnesota bar in 1857. In 1866 he had moved to Vicksburg to practice law with his brother, A. B. Pittman.

All the judges, including the chancellors and the state supreme court justices, had been appointed by

Governor James L. Alcorn from his Republican followers. Governor Alcorn was well known to be a very bitter political and personal enemy of Jefferson Davis because Davis had thwarted Alcorn's aspirations to a high commission in the Confederate Army. In 1870, Alcorn appointed Edwin Hill as Chancery Judge for Warren County. Hill, a native of Vermont, had been admitted to law practice in New York. After the Civil War he had moved to Vicksburg. Presumably the New Englander would not be very sympathetic with the Ex-Confederate President.

Aware of all the risks involved but with little to lose, Jefferson Davis filed suit in the Chancery Court of Warren County, Mississippi, on June 15, 1874 to establish title and recover *Brierfield*. Davis claimed that Joseph had given *Brierfield* to him. He recounted how he had entered the land, cleared and developed it, and openly used and adversely possessed it exclusively as his very own since 1835. It was alleged that in Jefferson's absence Joseph was to act as Jefferson's agent. Davis explained that the sale to the Montgomerys was subject to his ratification, which he had given. Jefferson also asserted that when Joseph had received payments from Ben Montgomery he had promptly made remissions to Jefferson for his proper share. Jefferson's petition prayed for his proportionate share of the payments received from Montgomery.

He asked that Ben Montgomery be allowed to rescind the purchase and return *Brierfield* to Jefferson Davis, its rightful owner.

Defendants were Dr. Bomar and J. D. Smith, Executors; Joseph D. Mitchell; Mrs. Mary Elizabeth Mitchell Hamer and her husband William D. Hamer; Benjamin Thornton Montgomery and sons, W. Thornton and Isaiah T., along with Jefferson's own children as nominal parties since they had been specified for bequests. The principal defendants were Lize Hamer and her brother, Joseph Mitchell. Representing Lize and Joseph Mitchell were three of the finest lawyers ever to practice in Mississippi: Wiley P. Harris, J. Z. George, and Thomas A. Marshall. All were loyal and patriotic Mississippians and admirers of the former Confederate President; George and Harris had both been Confederate officers.

The defense strongly contended that Joseph Davis had never parted with title to *Brierfield*, that Jefferson used the place by Joseph's permission and suffrance, and that Jefferson Davis' possession was with the consent of Joseph and not adverse. With firm insistence, the defendants charged that Jefferson was estopped to set up title in himself because of inconsistent conduct recognizing Joseph's ownership. They asserted that Jefferson had placed himself in a position where he could not justly deny Joseph Davis' title to *Brierfield*.

Ordered, Adjudged, and Decreed

Harris and George pulled no punches against their old leader. Pointed arguments were advanced in such harsh words as "double dealing," "concealment," "cruel misleading." [5] It was charged that he acted inconsistently with a "step deliberately (taken) with full knowledge" after "he had determined to acquiesce in it." [6] Extensive testimony was taken. Members of the family, neighbors, officials, and many other persons were witnesses. The evidence conflicted on several important points. Jefferson, however, was legally prevented from testifying to establish his own claim against his deceased brother's estate.

On January 8, 1876, Chancellor Edwin Hill dismissed Jefferson's suit, holding that Jefferson Davis, the "Complainant is estopped from maintaining this suit." [7] A somewhat drab appearing future now looked even darker for Jefferson Davis. Prospects for appeal were not bright. On the Supreme Court sat three unsympathetic Republican justices. A flicker of timely hope was ignited when one Supreme Court Justice, under vigorous public and legislative pressure, resigned and another declined to seek re-election. In their places two former Democrats and Confederate officers, both warm admirers of Jefferson Davis, were

[5] *Ibid.*, pp. 734, 738.
[6] *Ibid.*, p. 739.
[7] Warren County, Miss., Chancery Court, Minute Book 3, p. 117.

named to the court. Upon advice of counsel, Davis decided to appeal.

At this time, after a temporary residence with friends in New Orleans, Davis, in January, 1877, accepted the generous invitation of Mrs. Sarah Dorsey, a family friend, to reside at *Beauvoir* on the Gulf Coast. While the appeal was pending, executors of the Joseph Davis Estate filed suit to foreclose the Ben Montgomery mortgage on *Hurricane* and *Brierfield*. Four years after the original suit to reclaim *Brierfield* was filed, the Supreme Court at the April 1878 Term, by a vote of two to one, reversed Chancellor Hill's decision and ruled in favor of Jefferson Davis. At last Davis held title to his beloved *Brierfield*, subject only to the Montgomery sale and mortgage.

The victory was reassuring to the aging Davis. The court voted him a ringing vindication. All questions regarding his conduct were favorably resolved and completely justified. The court held that Jefferson's claim of adverse possession had been conclusively proved. He was deemed not guilty of any acts "indicative of personal dishonor"[8] nor had he misled or deceived anyone. Furthermore, he had caused no loss to anyone. At most, Jefferson had just changed his mind without harm to others. Although Chief Justice H. F. Simrall emphatically dissented, the opinions of Judges J. A. P. Campbell and H. H. Chalmers prevailed.

[8] Davis v. Bomar, 55 Mississippi Reports, p. 776.

Ordered, Adjudged, and Decreed

At memorial exercises for the Confederate leader, Justice Campbell spoke highly of Jefferson Davis when he asserted: "He was a great man. He was the grandest man I ever knew, and I hope I will be pardoned for saying that I have had opportunities for measuring him by some of the greatest of earth. Tried often, and on great occasions, he always proved equal to the demand upon him, and thus sustained the real test of greatness. . . . His faults, whatever they may have been, were eclipsed by his splendid virtues." [9]

Following the success of Jefferson Davis' appeal, the Warren County Chancery Court on June 1, 1878, entered a decree authorizing foreclosure of the Montgomery mortgage which was in default.[10] Enforcement was delayed by an appeal; not until March 5, 1881, was the way finally cleared for foreclosure. The court-directed sale was conducted on September 12, 1881,[11] and at long last on December 1, 1881, a deed to *Brierfield* was executed to Jefferson Davis and his only surviving children, Varina (Winnie) and Margaret Hayes.[12] After many years, the land became his without question. Jefferson Davis re-entered possession as master of *Brierfield*.

[9] J. William Jones, *The Davis Memorial Volume*, p. 667.
[10] Warren County, Miss., Chancery Court, Minute Book 3, p. 411.
[11] *Ibid.*, Minute Book 4, pp. 75, 85, 145.
[12] Warren County, Miss., Land Records, Deed Book ZZ, p. 529.

CHAPTER XI

Final Adieu

WHILE AT *Beauvoir* during April, 1881, Jefferson Davis dictated the final chapter of his *Rise and Fall of the Confederate Government*. Two large volumes were published in June of that year. Meanwhile, he and Varina had planned a trip to Europe with the intention of accompanying their seventeen year old daughter Winnie on her return home. They sailed from New York on August 17 and returned December 7, about the time that all steps for repossession of *Brierfield* were completed. Jefferson Davis at this time also owned *Beauvoir*. He had purchased the property from Mrs. Dorsey and made one payment before her death. In her will she forgave the remaining balance and left *Beauvoir* and other properties to Davis.

The mighty Mississippi River is always unpredictable and often cruel. As it had challenged the Montgomerys, the river now promptly created further problems for the surviving Davis brother. Heavy rains in the Ohio and Upper Mississippi valleys during January and February sent two great waves of high water against the sodden, inadequate, and poor maintained levees. The flood of 1882 was among the most destructive ever to occur on the Mississippi River.

Because he was apprehensive about *Brierfield*, Davis in April, 1882, made his first visit to the plantation since he had been re-established as its active owner. In mid-May, he and Varina returned together to survey the damage and render all possible assistance to the workers and tenants. O. B. Cox was Davis' first farm manager. Later Beckett Howell, Varina's younger brother, was placed in charge; but he died after managing the farm for only a few months.

In 1883 another damaging flood washed through the valley. Then, as if intent on delivering a knockout blow, the Mississippi River again went on the rampage after heavy precipitation in the Mississippi Basin during 1884. The roaring torrent was comparable to the formidable flood of 1882. Once more in 1886 high water caused misery and destruction. Nevertheless, the aging Ex-President, with the loyal aid of his dependable son-in-law, Addison Hayes, stubbornly and bravely battled these reverses.

So much work was necesary to keep the plantation productive that little other than bare essentials could be considered in maintaining the Big House. The plantation manager lived there, and a room was always kept ready for Jefferson Davis. From *Brierfield*, Jefferson wrote, "One trouble has chased another like waves, each being the herald of one to come." [1] Uncertain tenants, failing levees, incompetent and sometimes drunken overseers (with several notable exceptions), and sparse crops all plagued the weary owner. Yet he peremptorily rejected any thought of selling all or part of *Brierfield*.

During the first week of November, 1889, feeling reasonably well despite his eighty-one years, Davis left *Beauvoir* for *Brierfield*, where he expected to conclude settlements with his manager and tenants for the year. Although Varina insisted on accompanying him, he rather positively refused to let her make the journey with him. The weather turned cold as Jefferson passed through New Orleans. Exposed to rain and sleet, he caught cold and developed fever and severe bronchitis. By the time his steamboat reached *Brierfield*, Davis was seriously ill and almost delirious.

His last letter was written from *Brierfield* on November 12, 1889. Pitifully sick, distressed, and weak, he scribbled a barely intelligible note to Varina telling her he would return next day on the boat to New Orleans if he could get to the landing. He hoped she would not be alarmed and concluded, "I have suffered much. . . . Nothing is as it should be, and I am not able even to look at the place." [2] Several days of

---

[1] Strode, *Jefferson Davis: Private Letters*, p. 536.
[2] *Ibid.*, p. 561.

faithful and attentive care in the home he had completed almost forty years before failed to restore Davis' strength. The noble, brave, unyielding, and unpardoned old man was fighting his last battle within the walls of his beloved *Brierfield*.

By sheer will, the broken and failing veteran summoned strength enough to depart for New Orleans on Captain Leathers' southbound steamer. On November 13, 1889, the plantation agent, John C. Trainor, and his little niece helped Jefferson prepare for the return journey. Through dim eyes, the master of *Brierfield* looked about the simply furnished house which had been built with much love and toil during better days.

Hudson Strode has related that as Jefferson Davis was about to leave the house, Alice Desmaris, Trainor's ten year old niece, "timidly presented her album for his autograph and a sentiment." [3] Maintaining the essence of courtesy and gentleness even under the most adverse circumstances, Davis patiently, thoughtfully, and deliberately penned the last words he would ever write. Acutely conscious that he was at the place he had always loved and considered to be his home, he traced out the following words:

Brierfield, 13th Nov. 1889
May all your paths be peaceful and pleasant

[3] *Ibid.*

charged with the best fruit, the doing good to others.

Jefferson Davis[4]

Was this a message to one little girl, or was it a prayer for all the people he had known and served and led?

After returning his pen to the table, Jefferson, aided by loving hands, made his way through the broad middle hall of *Brierfield*, paused at the great doorway to the porch, then descended the steps to the carriage which was waiting to take him to the landing. He must have noticed the remnants of white cotton still in the fields so long ago cleared and the leaves falling from the tall woodland trees. The final winter season for land and life was fast approaching.

The bent and lonely figure was taken on board Captain Leathers' glistening boat. The weathered old riverman perhaps recalled the day years before when this same Jefferson Davis had boarded his vessel destined for Montgomery, Alabama, and leadership of the Confederacy. The great paddle wheel made the amber water foam as a deep blast from the steam whistle lifted a proud white plume, appropriate symbol of a gallant knight. The sound could be heard for miles around—a respectful salute, a cry of love, a moan of sorrow, a plaintive, lonely lament addressed to *Brierfield* and reminiscent of the message Jefferson Davis

[4] *Ibid.*

left with the Senate in 1861: "... it only remains for me to bid you a final adieu." [5]

On December 6, 1889, Jefferson Davis, master of *Brierfield*, died in New Orleans.

---

[5] Varina Howell Davis, *Jefferson Davis, Ex-President*, I, 696.

CHAPTER XII

Gone With the Bend

JEFFERSON DAVIS' will, written February 20, 1886, provided:

> I give and bequeath to my Wife Varina Davis, all of my personal belongings, including library, furniture, correspondence and the Brierfield plantation (proper) with all its appurtenances, being and situated in the County of Warren, State of Mississippi, and being the same on which we lived and toiled together for many years from the time of our marriage.[1]

Mrs. Davis depended on her capable son-in-law, Addison Hayes, husband of her daughter Margaret, to attend to the plantation business.

Late in 1888, upon recommendation of his New Orleans cotton brokers, Jefferson Davis had interviewed at *Beauvoir* the operator of a small Louisiana cotton farm. A. B. Couvillon, "a large, handsome man

[1] Warren County, Miss., Office of the Chancery Clerk, Will Book D, p. 365.

and a very gentlemanly person," [2] was employed as manager of *Brierfield* and moved there with his family that winter. He remained on the plantation for twenty-eight years until 1916, when the property was rented for pasturage and all farming operations were discontinued. The increasingly frequent and damaging floods which covered the property in 1890, 1892, 1893, 1897, 1903, 1907, 1912, 1913, 1916, and 1920 made farming more and more difficult.

Addison Hayes, from his home in Colorado Springs, Colorado, visited *Brierfield* at various times during each year, usually in the fall at cotton picking and ginning time. Frequently, his daughter Lucy and his son Jefferson Hayes-Davis would accompany him. As she grew older, Varina did not attempt to visit the plantation, but stayed with friends in Vicksburg while the men attended to the plantation business. Mr. Couvillon would travel to Vicksburg to consult with Mrs. Davis.

During Mr. Couvillon's management of the plantation, the pantry in the kitchen wing was used as a postoffice, since Mr. Couvillon also acted as postmaster. The east end was converted into a school room for the children of families residing on the island. Mrs. James D. Hitt and Mrs. Harry Doyle, two of the teachers employed during this period, traveled back and forth from Vicksburg on the steamer *Senator*

[2] Albert F. Ganier, letter to the author, January 12, 1966.

Cordill. Mrs. Hitt long remembered "the lighted reflection of the boat in the River, a weird but pretty sight," and the boat whistles that "could be heard at least two hours before they reached the landing." Because of changes in the course of the river, the house at *Brierfield* was now located about seven miles from the boat landing. The teacher recalled that the "road was quite woodsy and narrow, but kept quite passable." [3]

After Varina Davis died in 1906 and Joel Addison Hayes in 1919, Jefferson Hayes-Davis manfully assumed operation of *Brierfield* for the Davis heirs. At best, the task was not easy, and the long distance from Colorado to Mississippi added to his problems. In spite of the valiant efforts of Jefferson Hayes-Davis, the burden of maintenance and repair became almost intolerable.

From about 1921 to 1924, Henry Bobb served as manager of *Brierfield* and lived in the big house with his wife Verna. They always kept a room ready for Jefferson's grandson. In 1922, a flood in the lower river valley exceeded all previous records. The water rose halfway up the front porch columns and was at least six feet deep inside the house. In a desperate effort to save the sturdy old house, Jefferson Hayes-Davis in 1924 had the building raised ten feet above

[3] Mrs. James D. Hitt, written comments about *Brierfield* in the possession of the author.

the ground on brick pillars. This project was most difficult to execute.

Three years later in 1927, the overloaded Mississippi swirled to disastrous heights never before reached in all river history. According to Negroes living on the place, the muddy water lapped within reach of the raised joists but lacked one foot of getting into the house. The decision to raise *Brierfield* had been timely and justified.

After Henry Bobb left *Brierfield*, G. D. Gatewood lived in the house and managed the plantation. Although time and the abuse of war had not yet destroyed *Brierfield*, fierce natural elements seemed bent on its obliteration. During the last week of March, 1931, the wind was typically strong and gusty, the weather sunny and brisk. Jim Barnett, now an elderly Negro, was at the house on the day *Brierfield* burned. He recalls that a woman who worked on the place was ironing in the large north room which had been the master bedroom when the Davises occupied *Brierfield*. A young Negro girl who was helping to heat irons at the fireplace put some shingles on the fire in the grate. The strong draft sucked the light weight, burning pieces up through the chimney, and embers fell on the ancient wood-shingled roof, setting it on fire. Jim Barnett and others hastened to the top of the house with buckets of water and almost succeeded in arresting the flames, but they could not supply enough water to put out the fire. Whipped by the wind, the blaze roared out of control.[4]

The great frame structure, hewn from the woods and built with love and care, had endured for many decades; but the flames raged wildly through the airy rooms of *Brierfield*. In one last grand agony, *Brierfield* blazed high into the sky above as if finally released to join its builders. The smoke disappeared and the ashes settled. Amid a strange and vacant silence stood the bare, stark, empty pillars and chimneys of *Brierfield*.

Various dates have been given for the burning of *Brierfield*. Albert F. Ganier, a distinguished engineer of Nashville, Tennessee, great grandson of Amanda Davis Bradford, sister of Jefferson and Joseph Davis, and a careful, diligent student of the Davis family and Davis Bend, asserts, "Brierfield was burned the last week in March 1931."[5] Although others have dated the destruction in 1930 or 1932, Mr. Ganier is undoubtedly correct. The Memphis *Commercial Appeal* published a picture of *Brierfield* in the rotogravure section for Sunday, April 5, 1931, with the comment that the home "was destroyed by fire two weeks ago." An article by the Honorable Dennis Murphree, former governor of Mississippi, also reports the burning.[6] Aerial photographs taken by the United States

[4] Interview with James Barnett.

[5] Ganier, letter to the author, January 12, 1966.

[6] *The Commercial Appeal* (Memphis, Tenn.), April 5, 1931, Sec. IV, p. 8; and picture in rotogravure section, same date. *The*

Gone With the Bend

Engineers at Vicksburg in September, 1931, show the foundation piers of *Brierfield*. The house is gone.

After the big house burned, a small four room cabin was built on top of some of the old pillars. One or two additional brick piers were constructed to help support the cabin. The older pillars were mortared and repaired at that time. Scratched in the mortar smeared on the old foundation underneath the house is the following inscription:

W. V. Miller
Plasterer and Bricklayer
Oct. 21, 1931
of Vicksburg

Miller was one of the workmen sent to build the cabin on the ruins. His signature dates that construction. The little house perched on the middle pillars also burned a year or so after it was built. This later fire has probably been confused with the one which destroyed the old house. At any rate, the several published articles indicating that *Brierfield* was burned in 1932 are undoubtedly incorrect.

Distance, decay, deluge, and destruction finally presented difficulties too great to overcome. Jefferson Hayes-Davis came from Colorado Springs as often as

Vicksburg Evening Post of March 29, 1931 contained the following announcement: "Word is received here that 'Brierfield,' the plantation home of Jefferson Davis, burns on Palmyra Island."

possible because he and the other heirs loved the place. At considerable sacrifice they clung tenaciously to this tangible link with their revered grandfather. At last the heirs reluctantly decided to sell *Brierfield*.

Jefferson and Varina Davis had six children: four sons and two daughters. The boys died at the ages of two, five, twelve, and nineteen—none reached maturity. One daughter, Winnie, who never married, died in 1898 when she was thirty-four. Margaret married Joel Addison Hayes and they had five children. Four survived her: Jefferson Hayes-Davis; Lucy White Davis, who married George B. Young; William Davis-Hayes; and Varina Hayes, who married Gerald Bertram Webb. Varina Hayes Webb left her interest in *Brierfield* to her husband Gerald B. Webb for life, and at his death the remainder went to her five children, Mrs. Varina Margaret Webb Bennett, Mrs. Frances Robine Webb Farnsworth, Mrs. Eleanor Leila Constance Webb Collins, Joel Addison Hayes Webb, and Gerald Bertram Webb, Jr., who died in 1947.

On April 3, 1953, the surviving heirs of Jefferson Davis conveyed *Brierfield* to William E. Parks of St. Joseph, Louisiana, and George D. Hayes of Clinton, Louisiana. The deed recited that the place contained 3,136 acres including accretions from the river. Parks and Haynes sold *Brierfield* to John Dale, Jr., and Lessley D. Dale, both of Vidalia, Louisiana, on May

18, 1954. The Dales now own the property and maintain it as a game preserve. They are outstanding lawyers and extensive property owners, excellent gentlemen, very considerate, and humbly conscious of the cherished memories lurking within the shade of the massive oaks.

The old river rolls and rolls and rolls, past the looping Bend around the island, past the shrinking fields, past the broken bricks, past the fragrant wild roses, maintaining his fabled silence; but make no mistake, "old times dar am not forgotten."

Selected Bibliography

BOOKS

Bearss, Edwin C. *Decision in Mississippi*. Little Rock, Ark.: Mississippi Commission on the War Between the States, 1962.
———. *Rebel Victory at Vicksburg*. Little Rock, Ark.: The Vicksburg Centennial Commemoration Commission, 1963.
Davis, Jefferson. *The Rise and Fall of the Confederate Government*. 2 vols. New York and London: Thomas Yoseloff, 1958.
Davis, Varina Howell. *Jefferson Davis, Ex-President of the Confederate States, A Memoir by His Wife*. 2 vols. New York: Belford Company, Publishers, 1890.
Garner, James Wilford. *Reconstruction in Mississippi*. Gloucester, Mass.: Peter Smith, 1964. Reprint of 1st ed. published by The Macmillan Company, 1901.
Hoehling, A. A., and the Editors of Army Times Publishing Company. *Vicksburg, 47 Days of Siege*. Englewood Cliffs, N. Y.: Prentice-Hall, Inc., 1969.
Jones, J. William. *Memorial Volume of Jefferson Davis*. Richmond, Va.: B. F. Johnson & Co., 1890.

Selected Bibliography

Jones, Katherine M. *The Plantation South*. Indianapolis, Ind. and New York: The Bobbs-Merrill Company, Inc., 1957.

Kane, Harnett T. *Bride of Fortune*. Garden City, N. Y.: Doubleday & Company, Inc., 1948.

Mahan, Alfred Thayer. *Campaign of the Civil War, the Gulf and Inland Waters*. New York: Jack Brussel, (N.D.). Publishers.

Miers, Eral Schenck. *The Web of Victory, Grant at Vicksburg*. New York: Alfred A. Knopf, 1955.

Overstreet, Webb. *Early Mississippi Bar Associations*. Jackson, Miss.: Mississippi Bar Foundation, 1966.

Rowland, Eron, *Varina Howell, Wife of Jefferson Davis*. New York: The Macmillan Company, 1927.

Simkins, Francis Butler. *History of the South*. New York: Alfred A. Knopf, 1956.

Smith, J. Frazer. *White Pillars*. New York: William Helburn, Inc., 1941.

Strode, Hudson. *Jefferson Davis: American Patriot*. New York: Harcourt, Brace and Company, 1955.

———. *Jefferson Davis: Confederate President*. New York: Harcourt, Brace and Company, 1959.

———. *Jefferson Davis: Private Letters 1823–1889*. New York: Harcourt, Brace & World, Inc., 1966.

———. *Jefferson Davis: Tragic Hero*. New York: Harcourt, Brace & World, Inc., 1964.

PERIODICALS

Bigelow, Martha Mitchell. "Vicksburg: Experiment in Freedom." *Journal of Mississippi History*, XXVI (February, 1964), 28–44.

Selected Bibliography

McKinney, John. "Gone with the River—Plantation of Jefferson Davis." *The Progressive Farmer* (Mississippi-Arkansas-Louisiana ed.), LXXII, No. 3 (March, 1957), 72 *et seq.*

Murphree, Dennis. "Brierfield." *South*, I, No. 6 (August 1945), 7.

————. "Hunting Wild Geese on Jefferson Davis' Island." *The Southern Sportsman*, III, No. 3 (October, 1938), 4.

————. "Hurricane and Brierfield, the Davis Plantations." *The Journal of Mississippi History*, IX (April, 1947), 98–107.

NEWSPAPERS

Cotton, Gordon. "Ruins of Jefferson Davis' Home." *Vicksburg Sunday Post*, June 2, 1968.

McIntire, Carl. "Davis' Old Warren Homes Wrapped in Undergrowth." *The Clarion-Ledger, Jackson Daily News*, Sunday, July 25, 1965.

Murphree, Dennis. " 'Brierfield,' Historic Home of Jeff Davis, Runied by Fire." *The Commercial Appeal* (Memphis, Tenn.), Sunday, April 5, 1931, Sec. IV, p. 8.

Port Gibson (Miss.) *Reveille*, September 29, 1932.

Vicksburg (Miss.) *Evening Post*. Civil War Centennial Edition, July 1, 1963.

MISCELLANEOUS

Elliott, D. O. "The Improvement of the Lower Mississippi River for Flood Control and Navigation." Mississippi River Commission, May 1, 1932, I, 103–114.

"Flood Control in the Lower Mississippi River Valley." Vicksburg, Miss.: Mississippi River Commission and U.S. Army Engineer Division, Lower Mississippi Valley, Corps of Engineers, August, 1968.

"Mississippi River Navigation." Vicksburg, Miss.: Mississippi River Commission and Lower Mississippi Valley Division Corps of Engineers, May, 1969.

Mississippi. Senate Journal of Mississippi Legislature. January 11, 1934. "Jefferson Davis." Address delivered by Edgar Wilson, Statuary Hall, Washington, D. C., June 2, 1931.

United States Army Engineers. Aerial photographs and maps. Office of United States Army Engineers, Vicksburg, Miss.

PUBLIC RECORDS

Jefferson Davis v. J. H. D. Bomar, Executor, et al., decision of the Supreme Court of Mississippi, April, 1878. 55 Mississippi Reports, pp. 671–814.

Warren County, Miss. Chancery Court. Probate Records in Estate of Joseph E. Davis, deceased, in Cause No. 2606.

Warren County, Miss. Chancery Court records. Docket entries in case of Jefferson Davis v. J. H. D. Bomar, et al., Cause No. 1164.

Warren County, Miss. Chancery Court. Will of Jefferson Davis in Probate Cause No. 9018. Will Book D, p. 365.

Warren County, Miss. Land Records. "Abstract of

Title for Jefferson Hayes-Davis, et al property, Warren County, Mississippi." Prepared by Miss Frances Crawford.

Warren County, Miss. Land Records. Deed from Jefferson Hayes-Davis et al to William E. Parks and George P. Haynes, dated April 3, 1953. Deed Book 302, p. 361.

Warren County, Miss. Land Records. Deed from Parks and Haynes to John Dale, Jr. and Lessley D. Dale, dated May 18, 1854. Deed Book 310, p. 577.

Warren County, Miss. Marriage Records.

Warren County, Miss. Minutes of the Chancery Court of Warren County, Mississippi, in Cause No. 1277, styled "Jefferson Davis, et al, vs. Benj. T. Montgomery, et al."

LETTERS

Bahmer, Robert H., Archivist, General Services Administration, Washington, D. C., to Congressman John Bell Williams, August 20, 1965.

Dabney, J. B., to the author, June 4, 1957.

Doyle, Mrs. Harry, to the author, September 25, 1965.

Elsbree, Hugh L., Director, Legislative Reference Service, The Library of Congress, Washington, D. C., to Senator John Stennis, June 25, 1965.

Ford, Mary Frances Murphree, to the author. Jackson, Miss., August, 1964.

Ganier, Albert F., to the author, Nashville, Tennessee, January 12, 1966.

Hayes-Davis, Jefferson, to the author. Colorado Springs, Colorado, July 21, 1966.

Parker, Elmer O., for Robert W. Krauskopf, Chief Army

and Navy Branch, General Services Administration, National Archives and Records Service, Washington, D. C., to the author, March 23, 1966.

Russell, V. Blaine, to the author, Vicksburg, Miss., August 22, 1964.

MEMORANDA

Hitt, Mrs. James D. Written comments about *Brierfield*.

Roach, Mrs. M. P. H. Dated August 22, 1897. Deposited in the Department of Archives and History, Jackson, Miss.

Appendix

THE GENEALOGY
OF THE DAVIS FAMILY

(Editorial note) The first three generations of Jefferson Davis' ancestors in America are listed by roman numerals, I, II, III. Members of the fourth generation, including Jefferson Davis, are listed by capital roman letters, A through J. The descendants of the fourth generation are presented by charts beginning with Joseph Emory Davis (A) in Chart Two. The descending lines from the fourth generation are indicated by arabic and italic numbers and lowercase letters, seventh through ninth in parentheses: 1—fifth generation; a—sixth; (*1*)—seventh; (*a*)—eighth; (i)—ninth. Three tenth generation decendants are indicated by (a). Notes to the charts appear at the end of the genealogy.

CHART ONE

I Evan Davis[1]	m.	Mary
b. prior to 1695	(*ca.* 1716)	d. Dec., 1758
d. prior to May, 1747		
	(6 children)	
II Benjamin		
d. prior to 1762		
William	m.	Christiana
d. prior to 1771		d. prior to 1775
Samuel	m.	Martha
d. Dec., 1759		
Hannah	m.	Jacob Dubree, Jr.[2]
	(Jan. 12, 1758)	d. prior to 1768
Joseph		
Evan[3]	m.	Mary Emory
b. *ca.* 1729		Williams
d. *ca.* 1758		
	(1 child:	
	Samuel Emory)	

127

Appendix

THE CHILDREN OF SAMUEL EMORY DAVIS

III Samuel Emory Davis[4] b. *ca.* 1756 d. July 4, 1824	m. (*ca.* 1783)	Jane Cook[5] b. *ca.* 1760 d. Oct. 3, 1845
	(10 children)	
A Joseph Emory b. Dec. 10, 1784 d. Sept. 18, 1870	m. (1) m. (2) (Oct. 5, 1827)	(unknown) Eliza Van Benthuysen[6] b. Jan. 23, 1811 d. Oct. 4, 1863
B Benjamin b. 1786 d. Oct. 22, 1827	m.	Aurelia Smith b. 1802 d. 1866
C Samuel Emory, Jr. b. *ca.* 1788 d. *ca.* 1835	m. (*ca.* 1818)	Lucy Throck- morton b. 1800
D Anna Eliza b. Sept. 1, 1791 d. Aug. 13, 1870	m. (1816)	Luther L. Smith b. 1770 d. Dec. 23, 1833
E Isaac Williams Davis b. Oct., 1792 d. prior to 1860	m.	Susannah Gartley b. 1794
F Lucinda Farrar b. June 5, 1797 d. Dec. 14, 1873	m.	Hugh Davis b. 1792 d. 1818
G Amanda b. Dec., 1799 d. 1881	m. (1819)	David Bradford b. Feb., 1796 d. Mar. 12, 1844
H Matilda b. 1800 d. Mar. 16, 1834	m.	Mr. Vaughan
I Mary Ellen b. 1806 d. May 2, 1824	m. (1820)	Robert Davis b. 1790 d. 1825/30
J Jefferson Finis b. June 3, 1808 d. Dec. 6, 1889	m. (1) (June 17, 1835)	Sarah Knox Taylor b. Mar. 6, 1814 d. Sept. 15, 1835

m. (2)   Varina Banks
(Feb. 26, 1845)   Howell
                b. May 7, 1826
                d. Oct. 16, 1906

CHART THREE

DESCENDANTS OF JOSEPH EMORY DAVIS[7] (A)
(3 children by [1])
(no children by Eliza Van Benthuysen)

1. Florida A. Davis[8]   m. (1)   David McCaleb
   b. Mar. 31, 1811   (Oct. 15, 1830)
   d. Jan. 18, 1891

                 (2)   Edmund C. Laughlin
            (July 17, 1848)   b. June 11, 1811
                         d. Sept. 9, 1889

2. Caroline Davis[9]   m. (1)   Thomas E. Robins
   b. 1819   (Dec. 17, 1842)
   d. after 1878

             m. (2)   Abram F. Leonard
           (Dec. 3, 1856)

3. Mary Lucinda[10]   m.   Charles J.
   b. May 1, 1821   (Feb. 5, 1838)   Mitchell[11], M.D.
   d. Nov. 22, 1846 | b. May 31, 1813
                | d. Feb., 1886

            (3 children)
a. Mary Elizabeth   m.   William D. Hamer
   (Lize) Mitchell | b. 1840
   b. Feb. 22, 1842 | d. 1880
   d. May 1, 1927 |
            (4 children)
(1) Joseph Davis Hamer
   b. and d. 1874

(2) Mary Lucinda   m.   John G. O'Kelley
   (Lucy) Hamer   (1900)
   b. 1876 |
   d. 1960 |
            (4 children)
(a) John G. O'Kelley, Jr.
   d. May 15, 1901

(descendants of Joseph Emory Davis [A], continued)

(*b*) John Beatty O'Kelley   m.   Helena Villere
    b. 1903   (1937)

(*c*) Elizabeth Hamer   m.   John E. Kerrigan
    O'Kelley   (1928)   d. 1960
    b. 1905

                   (2 children)

  (i) John Esmond
      Kerrigan, Jr.
      b. 1930

 (ii) Elizabeth Mitchell Kerrigan
      b. 1938

(*d*) William Hamer O'Kelley
    b. 1908

(*3*) William David Hamer
    b. Dec. 2, 1878
    d. Aug. 12, 1923

(*4*) Joanna Milner Hamer
    b. and d. 1880

 b. Capt. Joseph Davis
    Mitchell[12]
    b. Oct. 9, 1839
    d. Dec. 19, 1911

 c. Hugh Mitchell[13]
    b. 1843
    d. 1849

CHART FOUR

DESCENDANTS OF BENJAMIN DAVIS[14] (B)

(1 child)

1. Mary Ann Davis[15]
    b. Aug., 1825
    d. Apr. 13, 1828

CHART FIVE

DESCENDANTS OF SAMUEL EMORY DAVIS, JR.[16] (C)

(5 children)

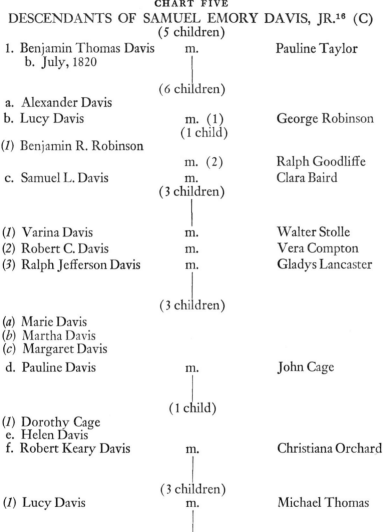

1. Benjamin Thomas Davis   m.   Pauline Taylor
    b. July, 1820

(6 children)

a. Alexander Davis
b. Lucy Davis   m. (1)   George Robinson
               (1 child)
(*1*) Benjamin R. Robinson

             m. (2)   Ralph Goodliffe
c. Samuel L. Davis   m.   Clara Baird
             (3 children)

(*1*) Varina Davis   m.   Walter Stolle
(*2*) Robert C. Davis   m.   Vera Compton
(*3*) Ralph Jefferson Davis   m.   Gladys Lancaster

(3 children)

(*a*) Marie Davis
(*b*) Martha Davis
(*c*) Margaret Davis
d. Pauline Davis   m.   John Cage

(1 child)

(*1*) Dorothy Cage
e. Helen Davis
f. Robert Keary Davis   m.   Christiana Orchard

(3 children)
(*1*) Lucy Davis   m.   Michael Thomas

(2 children)

(*a*) Marie Thomas
(*b*) Michael Thomas, Jr.

(descendants of Samuel Emory Davis, Jr. [C], *continued)*

(2) Marie Davis   m.   D. S. Fletcher

(3 children)

(a) Daniel Fletcher
(b) Robert R. Fletcher
(c) Wilfred Fletcher

(3) Winifred Davis

2. Helen Davis   m.   Maj. Patrick F.
   b. 1822   (Mar. 3, 1841)   Keary
        d. 1865/69

3. Robert H. Davis[17]
   b. 1824

4. Samuel A. Davis
   b. 1826
   d. 1827

5. Joseph Davis
   d. 20 years old

CHART SIX

DESCENDANTS OF ANNA ELIZA DAVIS[18]

(6 children)

1. Joseph Davis Smith[19]   m.   Mary Coralie
   b. Apr. 6, 1817   (Apr. 25, 1839)   Guibert[20]
   d. Jan. 13, 1876   b. 1822
        d. June, 1863

(11 children)

a. Mary Coralie Smith   m.   Richard James
   b. Dec. 19, 1839   (1859)   Nugent
   d. Sept. 1, 1869

(3 children)

(1) Ann Catherine Nugent   m.   Samuel T. Rhodes
   b. 1860
   d. 1937

(4 children)

(a) Samuel B. Rhodes

(*b*) Caroline **Nugent**
Rhodes
b. 1887
d. 1888

(*c*) Katherine **Nugent**
Rhodes

(*d*) Ima Rhodes
b. 1890
d. 1891

(2) Richard James   m.   Lillian Warfield
Nugent, Jr.[21]   (1890)
b. 1862
d. 1922
              (2 children)

(*a*) Richard James
Nugent III
b. 1893
d. 1922

(*b*) Harry Warfield   m.   Carolyn Wensel
Nugent   Carson
b. 1898

(*3*) Coralie G. Nugent   m.   John V. Lobdell[22]
b. 1867   (1887)
              (9 children)

(*a*) Richard Nugent
Lobdell

(*b*) Coralie Guibert
Lobdell

(*c*) John V. Lobdell III

(*d*) Florence Elizabeth
Lobdell

(*e*) Lillian Lobdell

(*f*) Mildred Lee Lobdell

(*g*) Anna Nugent Lobdell

(*h*) Ethel Elizabeth Lobdell

(*i*) Hugh Lewis Lobdell

b. Anna (Nannie)
Davis Smith
b. Sept. 6, 1841
d. 1938

133

Appendix

(descendants of Anna Eliza Davis [D], continued)

c. William Boyle   m.   Mary Ernestine
   Smith[23]   (1872)   Giraud
   b. Nov. 26, 1845   b. Apr. 11, 1852
   d. Feb. 24, 1919   d. June 20, 1919
               (13 children)

(1) Dona Ernestine Smith   m.   Augustus C.
   b. Sept. 15, 1872   (May 5, 1895)   De Grummond

               (3 children)

(a) Norma DeGrummond   m.   J. C. Houseman
   b. Mar. 2, 1896
   d. Dec., 1950

(b) Will White De Grummond   m.   Lena Young
   b. July 7, 1897   (Apr. 12, 1923)   b. Apr. 7, 1900
   d. Aug. 9, 1935

(c) Ernestine Augustus   m. (1)   Elizabeth Blair
   De Grummond   d. May, 1946
   b. Nov. 4, 1899
   d. Oct. 16, 1953

         m. (2)   Nancy Jane Lucas
         (Dec. 13, 1947)

(2) Mary Mathilde Smith   m.   James Turner
   b. 1874   Burke
   d. Nov. 22, 1902   d. June 13, 1914
               (2 children)

(a) Georgie Fabre Burke   m.   Rutledge S.
         (Sept. 18, 1923)   Thomas

(b) John Sebastian Burke   m.   Violet Irwin
   b. Feb. 2, 1901   (Oct. 21, 1925)
   d. Jan. 4, 1959

(3) Isabel Guibert Smith   m.   Samuel Seymore
   b. Jan. 1, 1876   (Apr. 29, 1896)   Braud
   d. Dec. 6, 1950   b. Jan. 22, 1871
               (3 children)   d. Jul. 29, 1958

(a) Felix Smith Braud   m.   Volida Loretta
   b. Sept. 24, 1897   (Mar. 19, 1921)   Hebert

(b) Dona Ernestine Braud   m.   John William
   b. Feb. 8, 1899   Wolf

(c) Woodie Nicholas Braud   m.   Addie Bourgeois
   b. Aug. 18, 1900   (Apr. 28, 1927)   b. May 31, 1902
   d. Feb. 14, 1967

Appendix

(4) Kemp Catlett Smith   m.   Laura Braud
    b. Feb. 28, 1878   (Jan. 21, 1897)   b. Sept. 5, 1875
    d. Nov. 1, 1955

    (5 children)

(a) Fitzroy Hampton Smith   m.   Gladys Robichaux
    b. Nov. 26, 1897   (Nov. 5, 1921)   b. July 30, 1902
    d. Nov. 15, 1949
(b) Gordon Frederick Smith   m. (1)   Ruth Carroll
    b. Mar. 23, 1899   (Sept. 1928)
       m. (2)   Mrs. Louvilla Ayer
       (Oct., 1944)   Dromgoole
(c) Glor Vina Ethel Smith
    b. Sept. 28, 1900
    d. in childhood
(d) Mary Ernestine Smith   m. (1)   Carl Landy
    b. Mar. 2, 1908
       m (2)   Roy Hays
       (June 10, 1936)
(e) Kemp Catlett Smith, Jr.   m.   Doris Barrilleaux
    b. Feb. 26, 1916   (1936)

(5) Valdemar Ernest Smith   m.   Florence O'Neill
    b. Oct. 18, 1880   (Apr. 30, 1907)
    d. 1969

    (11 children)
(a) Varina Davis Smith   m.   Dalton Lee Reid
    b. June 13, 1908   b. Apr. 10, 1904
       d. 1967
(b) Florence Isabel Smith   m.   Leon Bernard
    b. Nov. 4, 1909   Mayers
       b. Jul. 23, 1907
(c) Valdemar Ernest Smith, Jr.
    b. Sept. 11, 1911
    d. Aug. 23, 1913
(d) Fay Margaret Smith   m.   Lawrence T.
    b. May 8, 1913   Mathis
       b. Jan. 30, 1909
(e) Dorothy Elizabeth Smith   m.   Denis Isadore
    b. Aug. 5, 1915   (Sept. 16, 1936)   Mouton
       b. Apr. 4, 1916
       d. Nov. 16, 1962

Appendix

(descendants of Anna Eliza Davis [D], continued)

(f) Myrtle Helen Smith 　　b. Aug. 25, 1916	m.	Frank Leeroy 　Broussard
(g) Ella O'Neill Smith 　　b. Feb. 23, 1918	m.	Lawrence Hubert 　LeBlanc
(h) Florence Marjorie Smith 　　b. Oct. 12, 1919	m.	Frank Joseph 　Fava, Jr.
(i) Robert Emmett Smith 　　b. Sept. 23, 1920		
(j) Florence Agnes Smith 　　b. Jan. 18, 1922	m.	Charles Duval 　Caffery
(k) William Boyle Smith 　　b. Jan. 30, 1923	m.	Sophie Ann Trahan 　b. Jan. 28, 1940

(6) William Beauvais Smith   m.   Myrtle Lusk
     b. Jan. 30, 1884   (June 9, 1909)
                            |
                 (2 children)

(a) Jessie Lee Smith
     b. 1910
     d. 1912

(b) Jefferson Lusk Smith   m.   Ruth Zimmerman
     b. Jul. 9, 1913   (May 29, 1937)

(7) Jefferson Davis Smith   m.   Martie Bowland
     Lt. Com. USN   (Sept. 30, 1913)   d. Mar. 3, 1952
     b. Apr. 27, 1886
     d. June 26, 1940 |

                 (5 children)

(a) Martie Bowland Smith   m. (1)   Christopher
     b. Aug. 8, 1914   Butterworth

                  m. (2)   William F. Ferrier
(b) Jefferson Davis Smith, Jr.   m.   Evelyn Ann Baur
     Lt. Col. USMC   (Jul. 10, 1942)   b. Aug. 4, 1917
     b. Oct. 29, 1917

(c) Jessie Ernestine Smith
     b. Feb. 21, 1920
     d. in childhood

(d) William Bowland Smith
     b. Sept. 6, 1928
     d. in childhood

(*e*) Anne Purnell Smith   m.   Fred Cameron
    b. Sept. 25, 1935   (Sept. 10, 1955)   Jackson

(*8*) Coralie Guibert Smith   m. (1)   George Wesley
    b. Feb. 24, 1888   Proffitt
    d. Nov. 22, 1954   m. (2)   Carl Beatty
              (Nov. 17, 1919)   d. Nov. 9, 1952

             (1 child by [1])
(*a*) George Wesley Proffitt, Jr. m. (1)   Bonnie Belle Buck
    b. Mar. 25, 1912   m. (2)   Dorothy May

            (2 children by [2])
(*a*) Doris Eileen Beatty   m. (1)   Charles Hill Braud
    b. Jan. 24, 1921   m. (2)   Julius Deisze
            (Feb. 13, 1944)

(*b*) Mary Coralie Beatty   m.   Joseph George
    b. Mar. 15, 1923   (Feb. 13, 1943)   Kowalczu

(*9*) Joseph Davis Smith III   m.   Estelle Hopkins
    b. May 29, 1890   (Sept. 6, 1916)
    d. Apr. 2, 1956

            (1 child)
(*a*) Mary Smith   m.   John Fisher Wright
    b. Mar. 25, 1918   (Sept. 6, 1938)

(*10*) Beulah De Veriere Smith   m. (1)   Maurice B. Harrell
    b. June 19, 1894   m. (2)   Rhea N. Watts
            (Jul. 8, 1929)

(*11, 12, 13*)
    died in infancy.

d. Lucy B. Smith   m.   Capt. Louie G.
    b. Apr. 22, 1848   (Oct. 21, 1873)   Balfour
    d. Dec. 29, 1917
            (7 children)

(*1*) Lulu Balfour

(*2*) Gartley Balfour
    b. 1879
    d. 1918

(*3*) Mary Blackman
    Balfour

Appendix

(descendants of Anna Eliza Davis [D], continued)

(4) Hollie Balfour

(5) Mary Balfour

(6) Joseph Balfour

(7) Cora Balfour

e. Joseph Davis Smith, Jr.
   b. Apr. 20, 1852
   d. Dec. 6, 1900

 f. Auguste G. Smith
    b. Aug. 6, 1853
    d. July 30, 1868

g. Amanda Philander Smith b. Mar. 5, 1854 d. Jan. 6, 1926	m. (Oct. 1, 1877) | (5 children)	Stephen Cobb Stirling
(1) John Bryson Stirling	m. | (7 children)	Anna Barrow
(a) John B. Stirling, Jr.[24]	m.	Estelle Couvillion
(b) Anna Barrow Stirling d. Jan. 1965	m.	Jefry Walters
(c) Mary Maud Stirling	m.	Thomas Hale
(d) Gilliard Stirling	m. | (1 child)	M. R. Guell
(i) Marilyn Stirling		
(e) Jeff Davis Smith Stirling	m. | (1 child)	Ruth ——
(i) Barbara Stirling		
(f) Frank Winter Stirling d. 1955		
(g) Flora A. Stirling	m. (1) m. (2)	Carl J. Moreau Harry Shaffer

(2 children by [1])

(i) John Bryson Moreau
(ii) Carl J. Moreau, Jr.

(2 children by [2])

(i) Harrison Shaffer
(ii) Bobby Lee Shaffer

(2) Frank Stirling

(3) Mary Maud Stirling   m.   William Percy

(2 children)

(a) Nannie Percy   m.   Will Whetker
(b) John Herford Percy   m.   Jean Lipscomb

(3 children)

(i) Ann Percy
(ii) Katherine Percy
(iii) Mary Percy

(4) Jefferson Davis Stirling

(5) Nannie Stirling

h. Luther L. Smith III
    b. Jan. 1, 1857
    d. July 23, 1861

i. Jefferson Davis Smith
    b. Sept. 18, 1858
    d. Sept. 7, 1907

j. Gordon A. Smith II
    b. Jan. 31, 1860
    d. June 30, 1861

k. Helen Keary Smith
    b. June 29, 1863
    d. Dec. 31, 1878

2. Luther L. Smith, Jr.[25]
    b. 1818
    d. 1850

3. Gordon A. Smith
    b. 1820

4. Lucinda Jane Smith   m.   William D. Boyle
    b. 1822   (1838)

(descendants of Anna Eliza Davis [D], continued)

5. Jedediah D. Smith b. 1824	m.	Susan M. Buck

6. Anna Amanda[26]
  Davis Smith
  b. 1826
  d. *ca.* 1900
	m.
	(1850)
		Philander C. Smith

	(2 children)	
a. Anna Davis Smith b. 1853	m. (1) (1871)	Robert C. Smith
	m. (2)	William Gunning
b. (daughter)	m.	Dr. Bert E. Young

CHART SEVEN

DESCENDANTS OF ISAAC WILLIAMS DAVIS[27](E)

(2 children)

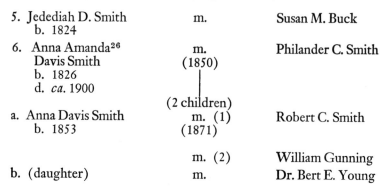

1. Infant son[28] d. 1824		

2. Joseph R. Davis[29]
  b. Jan. 12, 1825
  d. Sept. 15, 1896
	m. (1)
	(1848)
		Miss Peyton

	m. (2) (1879) (2 children by [2])	Margaret Green
a. Varina Jefferson Davis	m. (2 children)	Alphonse Marret
(*1*) Joseph Davis Marret b. 1913		
(*2*) Jefferson Marret d. infancy		
b. Edith Cary Davis	m. (1 child)	Jules C. L'Hote
(*1*) Jules C. L'Hote, Jr.		

DESCENDANTS OF LUCINDA FARRAR DAVIS[30] (F)

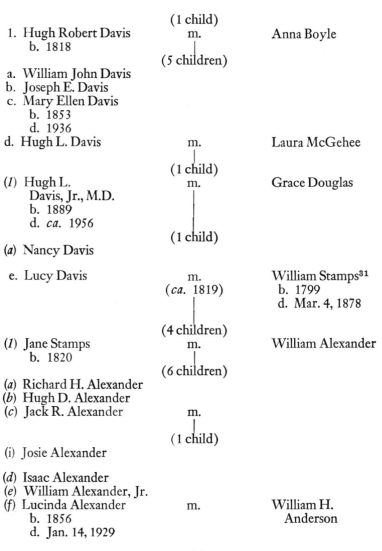

(1 child)

1. Hugh Robert Davis   m.   Anna Boyle
   b. 1818

(5 children)

a. William John Davis
b. Joseph E. Davis
c. Mary Ellen Davis
   b. 1853
   d. 1936
d. Hugh L. Davis   m.   Laura McGehee

(1 child)

(*1*) Hugh L.   m.   Grace Douglas
   Davis, Jr., M.D.
   b. 1889
   d. *ca.* 1956

(1 child)

(*a*) Nancy Davis

e. Lucy Davis   m.   William Stamps[31]
       (*ca.* 1819)   b. 1799
                     d. Mar. 4, 1878

(4 children)

(*1*) Jane Stamps   m.   William Alexander
   b. 1820

(6 children)

(*a*) Richard H. Alexander
(*b*) Hugh D. Alexander
(*c*) Jack R. Alexander   m.

(1 child)

(i) Josie Alexander

(*d*) Isaac Alexander
(*e*) William Alexander, Jr.
(*f*) Lucinda Alexander   m.   William H.
   b. 1856   Anderson
   d. Jan. 14, 1929

(descendants of Lucinda [F] continued)

(2) Anna Aurelia Stamps   m.   Claiborne Farish[32]
    b. 1823   (Jan. 17, 1856)   b. 1820

    (4 children)

(a) Hazelwood Farish
    b. 1856

(b) Lucinda (Lucy)   m.   Hugh Bradford
    Stamps Farish
    b. 1859

    (4 children)

 (i) Paul Bradford
 (ii) Lucy May Bradford
(iii) Stamps Bradford
(iv) Hugh Bradford, Jr.

(c) Isaac Stamps Farish
    b. 1861

(d) Elizabeth Jane
    (Varina) Farish
    b. 1865

(3) William Stamps, Jr.
    b. 1825
    d. 1842

(4) Isaac Davis Stamps[33]   m.   Mary Elizabeth
    b. Apr. 23, 1828   Humphreys[34]
    d. Jul. 1863

    (4 children)

(a) Lucinda (Lucy)   m.   Edgar Howard
    Davis Stamps   (1878)   Farrar[35]
                                       b. June 20, 1849
                                       d. Jan. 6, 1922

    (6 children)

 (i) Edgar H. Farrar, Jr.   m.

    (2 children)

(a) Isaac Stamps Farrar   m.   Maude White
(b) Maude Ellen Farar   m.   Mr. Kirkpatrick

 (ii) Mary Farrar   m.   Joseph Goldberger
(iii) Anna Farrar   m.   R. F. Goldsborough
    (4 children)

(iv) Lucinda Farrar
    d. 1911
(v) Edith Farrar
(vi) Jane Farrar   m.   Ralph B. Wood

                         (1 child)

(a) Jane Wood
(b) Mary McL. Stamps   m.   Charles E. Bateson

                  (3 children)

 (i) Mary Bateson   m.   Dr. Gillard
(ii) ?
(iii) ?
(c) Mildred Stamps
(d) Sallie Stamps

CHART NINE

DESCENDANTS OF AMANDA DAVIS[36](G)

(9 children)

1. David Bradford, Jr.[37]
    b. July. 25, 1821
    d. Aug. 15, 1836
2. Benjamin Franklin Bradford[38]
    b. 1822/23
    d. 1885
3. Mary Jane (Malie)   m. (1)   Richard Brodhead[40]
    Bradford[39]   (Apr. 3, 1849)   b. 1811
    b. 1825   d. 1863
    d. 1877

                  m. (2)   Robert Sayre
                  (1872)
           (2 children by [1])

a. Richard Brodhead, Jr.
    b. May 30, 1850
    d. Oct. 8, 1908
b. Jefferson Davis   m.   Cecile Harvier
    Brodhead

                  (3 children)

143

Appendix

(*1*) Ethel Mary Brodhead
(*2*) Leonie Brodhead
(*3*) Cecile Brodhead

4. Anna (Nancy)
   Matilda Bradford
   b. 1827
   d. 1904
	m.
	(May 17, 1848)
		Edward Lancaster
		   Miles
		   b. 1825
		   d. 1905

5. Jefferson Davis Bradford
   b. 1828
   d. 1910
	m. (1)
	m. (2)
		Helen Sumner
		Virgie Patterson

6. Lucinda (Lucy)
   S. Bradford
   b. Nov. 11, 1831
   d. Feb. 7, 1919
	m.
	(Dec. 13, 1850)
		Charles J.
		   Mitchell, M.D.[41]
		   b. May 31, 1813
		   d. Feb., 1886

(8 children)

a. Amanda Davis
   Mitchell
   b. Feb. 9, 1852
   d. Jan. 24, 1910
	m.
	(1877)
		Elie Ganier[42]
		   b. 1839
		   d. Oct. 4, 1903

(3 children)

(*1*) Elie Joseph Ganier[43]
     b. 1878
	m.	Ethel Gill
		   b. 1888

(4 children)

(*a*) Ethel Davis Ganier b. 1914	m. (2 children)
(*b*) Elie Ganier (twin) b. 1916	m. (1 child)
(*c*) Eugene Ganier (twin) b. 1916	m. (2 children)
(*d*) Lucy Lee Ganier	m. (2 children)

(*2*) Mitchell Louis Ganier
     b. 1880
     d. 1958
	m.
	(1907)
		Louise Cobb

3) Albert F. Ganier   m.   Anna Eastman
    b. Sept. 9, 1883   (1912)   b. 1887
                  (3 children)

a) Robert Eastman Ganier   m.
    b. May 13, 1913   (3 children)
b) Albert Franklin Ganier   m.
    b. Apr. 1, 1915   (3 children)
c) Anne Davis Ganier   m.
    b. Sept. 23, 1921   (3 children)

b. Mary Mitchell
    b. 1853
    d. 1854

c. Charles Mitchell
    b. Aug. 9, 1855
    d. Nov. 15, 1913

d. Maunsell Joseph   m.   Mary Rose
    Mitchell[44]   Lancaster
    b. Nov. 14, 1860   b. 1862
    d. Dec. 23, 1893   d. 1939
                  (1 child)

(*1*) Maunsell Mitchell
    b. 1883

e. Anna Mitchell
    b. and d. 1863

f. Alexander T.   m.   Columbia Flannigan
    Mitchell, M.D.   b. 1873
    b. 1865   d. 1964
    d. 1905

g. David Nugent Mitchell
    b. Mar. 2, 1870
    d. Sept. 3, 1874

h. Francis Xavier Mitchell
    b. 1860
    d. 1870

7. David Bradford   m.   Ada E. Pottinger
    b. 1835   b. 1854
    d. 1903   d. 1884

Appendix

(descendants of Amanda Davis [*G*]*, continued)*

8. Elizabeth (Betty) Parker Bradford b. 1831 d. 1917	m. (June 12, 1855) (11 children)	Maunsell White II[45] b. 1830 d. 1896
a. Maunsell White III b. 1856		
b. Lucinda White b. 1858	m. (1886) (4 children)	Clement P. Wilkinson, M.D.

(*1*) Maunsell White
  Wilkinson
(*2*) Clement Wilkinson
(*3*) Edward Wilkinson
(*4*) Bettie Wilkinson

c. Mary Bradford White b. 1862	m. (1889) (5 children)	Ringold Broussard b. 1831

(*1*) Edward Broussard
(*2*) Maunsell Broussard
(*3*) Ringold Broussard
(*4*) Mary Broussard

(*5*) Sidney Lee Broussard	m.	Henry Hardin
d. Carl Bradford White b. 1864 d. 1931	m. (7 children)	Mary Mitchell b. 1872

(*1*) Mary Elizabeth White
  b. 1891

(*2*) Nancy White b. 1892	m.	C. E. Johnson

(*3*) Carl B. White
  b. 1894
(*4*) Richard White
  b. 1896
(*5*) Charlotte White
  b. 1898

6) Maunsell White
   b. 1900
7) Lincoln White
   b. 1902

  e. Albert Sidney   m.   Mary Ellen Tobin
       Johnson White
       b. 1866

                (5 children)

(1) Maunsell White
(2) Albert Sidney White
(3) Ellen White
(4) Elizabeth White
(5) Maud White

  f. Elizabeth (Elise)   m.   Edward Robb
       Parker White

  g. Nancy Miles White   m.   Thomas Anderson

                (2 children)

(1) Lucy Anderson
(2) Thomas Anderson, Jr.

  h. Jeane White

  i. Eloise White
       b. 1868
       d. 1872

  j. De La Rond White
       b. and d. 1863

  k. David Bradford White
       b. 1860
       d. 1876

  g. Sarah Aurelia D. Bradford
       b. 1833
       d. 1852

CHART TEN

MATILDA DAVIS (H)

(no known children)

Appendix

CHART ELEVEN
DESCENDANTS OF MARY ELLEN DAVIS[46](I)

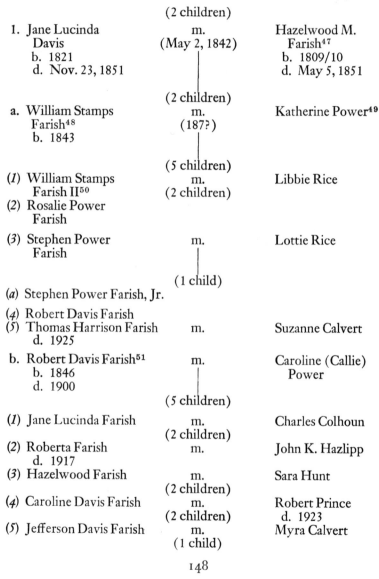

(2 children)

1. Jane Lucinda   m.   Hazelwood M.
Davis   (May 2, 1842)   Farish[47]
b. 1821   b. 1809/10
d. Nov. 23, 1851   d. May 5, 1851

(2 children)

a. William Stamps   m.   Katherine Power[49]
Farish[48]   (187?)
b. 1843

(5 children)

(1) William Stamps   m.   Libbie Rice
Farish II[50]   (2 children)
(2) Rosalie Power
Farish

(3) Stephen Power   m.   Lottie Rice
Farish

(1 child)

(a) Stephen Power Farish, Jr.

(4) Robert Davis Farish
(5) Thomas Harrison Farish   m.   Suzanne Calvert
d. 1925

b. Robert Davis Farish[51]   m.   Caroline (Callie)
b. 1846   Power
d. 1900

(5 children)

(1) Jane Lucinda Farish   m.   Charles Colhoun
       (2 children)
(2) Roberta Farish   m.   John K. Hazlipp
d. 1917
(3) Hazelwood Farish   m.   Sara Hunt
       (2 children)
(4) Caroline Davis Farish   m.   Robert Prince
       (2 children)   d. 1923
(5) Jefferson Davis Farish   m.   Myra Calvert
       (1 child)

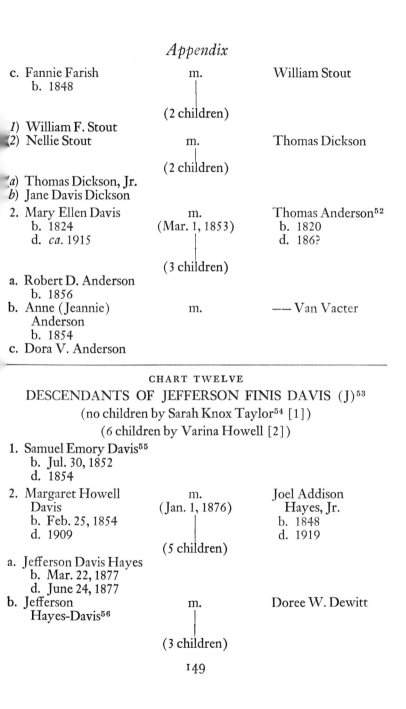

c. Fannie Farish   m.   William Stout
   b. 1848

                         (2 children)

1) William F. Stout
2) Nellie Stout   m.   Thomas Dickson

                         (2 children)

a) Thomas Dickson, Jr.
b) Jane Davis Dickson
2. Mary Ellen Davis   m.   Thomas Anderson[52]
   b. 1824   (Mar. 1, 1853)   b. 1820
   d. *ca.* 1915   d. 186?

                         (3 children)

a. Robert D. Anderson
   b. 1856
b. Anne (Jeannie)   m.   —— Van Vacter
   Anderson
   b. 1854
c. Dora V. Anderson

CHART TWELVE

DESCENDANTS OF JEFFERSON FINIS DAVIS (J)[53]

(no children by Sarah Knox Taylor[54] [1])

(6 children by Varina Howell [2])

1. Samuel Emory Davis[55]
   b. Jul. 30, 1852
   d. 1854

2. Margaret Howell   m.   Joel Addison
   Davis   (Jan. 1, 1876)   Hayes, Jr.
   b. Feb. 25, 1854   b. 1848
   d. 1909   d. 1919

                         (5 children)

a. Jefferson Davis Hayes
   b. Mar. 22, 1877
   d. June 24, 1877
b. Jefferson   m.   Doree W. Dewitt
   Hayes-Davis[56]

                         (3 children)

(1) Jefferson Hayes-
    Davis, Jr.
(2) Addison Hayes-Davis
(3) Adele Hayes-Davis

  c. Lucy White Hayes   m.   George Beyer
     b. 1882   Young
                     (5 children)

  d. Varina Howell Hayes   m.   Gerald Bertram
     b. 1879   Webb, M.D.

                     (5 children)

(1) Varina Margaret Webb m.   Gerald Bennet
(2) Frances Robine Webb   m.   Mr. Farnsworth
(3) Eleanor Lelia
    Constance Webb   m.   Mr. Collins
(4) Joel Addison Hayes Webb
(5) Gerald Bertram Webb, Jr.
    d. 1947

  e. William Davis Hayes   m.   Elizabeth Davis
     b. 1889

                     (2 children)

(1) Elise Hayes
(2) William Davis Hayes

  3. Jefferson Finis Davis, Jr.[57]
     b. Jan. 16, 1857
     d. Oct. 16, 1876

  4. Joseph Evan Davis[58]
     b. 1859
     d. Apr. 30, 1864

  5. William Howell Davis[59]
     b. Dec. 16, 1861
     d. Oct. 16, 1873

  6. Varina Ann (Winnie) Davis[60]
     b. June 27, 1864
     d. Sept. 18, 1898

---

[1] Evan Davis, the elder, great grandfather of Jefferson Davis, was a Welsh-man who immigrated to Philadelphia. A deed dated September 30, 1734, is the earliest record of his residence there. His will, made in 1843, gave his youngest sons, Joseph and Evan, a larger part of his estate.

Appendix

2 Dubree administered his father-in-law's estate.

3 Evan, the younger, Jefferson Davis' grandfather, moved from Philadelphia, rst to South Carolina, then to Georgia, where he married Mary Williams, nee .mory.

4 Samuel, the only child of Evan, the younger, was the father of Jefferson ~avis. He died at Davis Bend and was buried at *Hurricane*. His body was removed ɔ *Beauvoir* in 1940.

5 Jane Cook was the daughter of Mr. Cook who married Jeannie Strahan of ·cotland. She is buried at *Rosemont*.

6 Eliza Van Benthuysen from New Orleans was of a New York Dutch family also spelled Bentheson, Bentheyson, and Benthyson). She was an invalid most of •er life. She died at Lauderdale Springs, Mississippi, seeking safety after the fall of ⁄icksburg. In *Hurricane* cemetery are buried Jane E. Davis Nicholson, born in ·818, and her husband, Anderson Davis Nicholson, born in 1816. They married in ·842, and Jefferson Davis signed their marriage bond, implying that one or both ⁄ere of the Davis household. Jane died February 5, 1845, and Anderson on Febru- ·ry 3, 1846. The family relationship, if any, is not known. The names indicate a onnection. Dr. Strode mentions that a Joe Nicholson in 1863 was said to be a •ephew of Mrs. Eliza Davis. Joe could have been a son of Jane and Anderson. In orrespondence after the war, Joe Nicholson addressed Joseph E. Davis (A) as 'grandfather."

7 Early personal family information about Joseph E. Davis is scant, partly due ɔ his private wishes and also because of his known disinterest in genealogical ·ecords.

An unusual incident illustrates the spirit of generosity and warm hospitality that ·revailed at *Hurricane* under the dominant humanity of Joseph. Martha Louise ⟩uartes was the daughter of Judge John Turnstall Quartes of Russellville, ⟨entucky, old friend of the Joe Davis family. At an early age, Martha Louise's ⟩arents and her grandfather died, leaving her an orphan under the care of her vidowed grandmother Wallace. While Mrs. Wallace and Martha Louise were ɔn a visit to *Hurricane*, the grandmother became ill and died. Joseph Davis' •ousehold accepted the young girl into its warm circle, and she became "a herished and beloved daughter." She was educated in her native Kentucky and narried Horatio J. Harris, auditor of the state of Indiana, and later a lawyer and Jnited States Attorney in Vicksburg. After her husband's death Martha became ·n invalid and suffered greatly. In his will, Joseph Davis bequeathed his "adopted ◄aughter" $1,000. Many thought her to be a niece or near relative. She died May ·5, 1889, and following her own request she was buried "beside her loved ones ·esting there" at *Hurricane*. After her funeral at St. Paul's Catholic Church in ⁄icksburg, her remains were accompanied down the river by friends and rela- ·ives aboard the steamer Goldman to Davis Island.

8 Florida Davis was given *Diamond Place* in Warren County.

9 Caroline Davis Leonard died at Williamsburg, Virginia.

10 Mary Lucinda died in Cuba where she had gone because of failing health.

11 Charles Jouett Mitchell, educated in Paris, was a Vicksburg physician. After Mary Lucinda's death, he married her first cousin, Lucinda S. Bradford.

12 Captain Joseph D. Mitchell was born in France.

13 Hugh Mitchell was killed when thrown from a horse.

Appendix

14 Benjamin Davis died of yellow fever at *Locust Grove*. His wife, Aurelia, was the only daughter of Courtland Smith and Catherine Cooper. Her father married four times, as did Aurelia herself. She spent her early childhood with her Uncle Philander Smith at *The Oaks*; her later girlhood was spent with her Uncle Luther Smith at *Locust Grove* where she preferred to make her home. She was the first graduate of Elizabeth Female Academy at Washington, Mississippi. After Benjamin Davis died, Aurelia married Maj. General E. W. Ripley, U.S. Army by whom she had Aurelia Wheelock Ripley. Both husband and child died in 1839 and are buried at *Locust Grove*. Her third husband was a cousin, Thomas Bell Smith (d. 1851), and their only child was Lucy Ann Smith, who was born in Jackson, Louisiana in 1840 and died in New Orleans in 1933. Aurelia's fourth husband, John Smith Woodward, survived her.

15 Mary Ann Davis died at *Locust Grove* and is buried there.

16 Samuel Emory Davis, Jr., was born in Wilkes County, Georgia.

17 Robert H. Davis served in the Confederate Army.

18 Anna Eliza Davis was born in Wilkes County, Georgia. Her husband, Luther L. Smith, was the son of Reverend Jedediah Smith of *Locust Grove*, who died in 1776, and Sara Cook Smith, who died in 1790.

19 Joseph Davis Smith with his brother Luther Smith, Jr., bought *Solitude* where Levi Sholars had built the original home in 1789. Mrs. Guibert, his wife's mother, previously owned and named *Solitude*; Dr. Smith added to the house in 1835.

20 Mary Coralie Guibert was the daughter of Augustus David Guibert who was born in Paris, France. He came to New Orleans from San Domingo during the French Revolution. In the War of 1812 he served in Major Plauchard's Battalion of Louisiana Volunteers in defense of New Orleans, 1814–15. In 1816/18 he married Miss Beauvais of Louisiana. Augustus David Guibert's mother was a DeVeriere.

21 Erroneously referred to as "William" in Joseph Davis' estate papers.

22 John V. Lobdell was from Rosedale, Mississippi.

23 William Boyle Smith, who served in Taylor's division, C.S.A., was educated in Switzerland after the war. His wife, Ernestine Giraud, was born in Paris, France.

24 At this writing John B. Stirling, Jr., 2961 Jessamine Avenue, Baton Rouge, Louisiana, is part owner of *Locust Grove*.

25 Luther Smith, Jr., who bought *Solitude* with his brother Dr. Joseph Smith never married.

26 Anna Amanda Smith married her cousin, Philander C. Smith, son of Philander Smith, a brother of Luther L. Smith.

27 Isaac Davis was born in Georgia. He moved to Davis Bend with his brother Joseph. Soon after they began to cultivate the place, a severe cyclone struck, destroying many improvements and doing much damage to the main house. Isaac received a broken leg, crippling him for life.

28 Infant son of Isaac killed in cyclone.

29 Joseph R. Davis, a lawyer of Biloxi, was a brigadier general on the staff of President Jefferson Davis.

30 Lucinda Farrar Davis was born in Christian County, Kentucky. Her husband, Hugh Davis, Wilkinson County, Mississippi, drowned in 1818. He was probably a brother of Robert Davis who married Mary Ellen Davis (Chart Eleven).

Appendix

31 William Stamps, born in Kentucky, was a planter and commission merchant at *Rosemont*.

32 Claiborne Farish, born in Virginia, was a lawyer in Wilkinson County, Mississippi.

33 Isaac Davis Stamps was killed at Gettysburg.

34 Mary Elizabeth Humphreys was the daughter of Governor B. G. Humphreys of Mississippi.

35 Edgar Howard Farrar was a distinguished citizen of New Orleans.

36 Amanda Davis was born in Christian County, Kentucky. Her husband, David Bradford, West Feliciana lawyer and planter, was the first superintendant of the U.S. Mint at New Orleans, 1837–39. He was killed from ambush, March 12, 1844.

37 David Bradford, Jr., is buried at *Hurricane*.

38 Benjamin F. Bradford, a bachelor, is buried at *Locust Grove*.

39 Mary Jane Bradford went to Washington, D.C., with Jefferson and Varina Davis in 1846.

40 Richard Brodhead was a U.S. Senator from Philadelphia, Pennsylvania.

41 Charles J. Mitchell's first wife was Mary Davis, daughter of Joseph Davis (A).

42 Elie Ganier was a Confederate veteran.

43 Elie Joseph Ganier became a planter at Hollandale, Mississippi.

44 Maunsell Mitchell was killed at Ursino Landing.

45 Maunsell White II was the son of Captain Maunsell White, Louisiana Blues, Major Plauche's Battalion, Battle of New Orleans.

46 Mary Ellen Davis is buried at *Rosemont*. Her husband, Robert Davis, son of Hugh Davis and Ellen Cautey, was probably a brother of Hugh Davis who married Lucinda Davis (F), Mary Ellen's sister.

47 Hazelwood Farish, a Woodville, Mississippi, lawyer, is buried at *Rosemont*.

48 William Stamps Farish, a resident of Vicksburg, served in the Confederate Army.

49 Katherine Power, of Natchez, was living in Houston, Texas, in 1926.

50 William Stamps Farish II, president and chairman of the board of Standard Oil Company of New Jersey, retired in the 1930's. He is buried in Houston, Texas.

51 Robert Davis Farish served in the Confederate Army.

52 Thomas Anderson was from LaFayette County, Mississippi.

53 Jefferson Davis, President of the Confederacy, was born at Fairview, Kentucky. He died in New Orleans.

54 Sara Knox Taylor was the daughter of Zachary Taylor, twelfth president of the United States. She is buried at *Locust Grove*.

55 Samuel Emory Davis died of a sudden fever.

56 His name was legally changed to Hayes-Davis.

57 Jefferson Davis, Jr., died in Memphis of yellow fever at age nineteen.

58 Joseph Evan Davis died in Richmond during the war, from a fall from a window, at five years of age.

59 William Howell Davis died at age twelve of diphtheria.

60 "Winnie" Davis, called the "daughter of the Confederacy," never married.

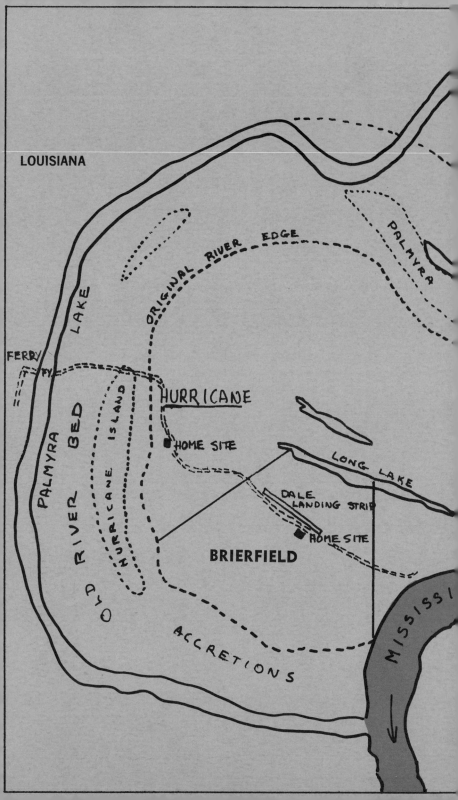